(AN OPERATING MANUAL)

JOHNNY DEEP

AS TOLD BY: ZEKE GEEK, THE GODDESS,
DILBART, FORREST GEEK, DALE CARNEGEEK,
AND MANY MORE . . .

ILLUSTRATED BY BRUCE TINSLEY AND RICH GABRIEL

THE
COMPLETE
GEEK
(AN OPERATING MANUAL)

BROADWAY BOOKS   NEW YORK

BROADWAY

The Complete Geek. Copyright © 1997 by John Deep. All rights reserved. Printed in the United States of America. No part of this book may be reproduced or transmitted in any form or by any means, electronic or mechanical, including photocopying, recording, or by any information storage and retrieval system, without written permission from the publisher. For information, address Broadway Books, a division of Bantam Doubleday Dell Publishing Group, Inc., 1540 Broadway, New York, NY 10036.

Broadway Books titles may be purchased for business or promotional use or for special sales. For information, please write to: Special Markets Department, Bantam Doubleday Dell Publishing Group, Inc., 1540 Broadway, New York, NY 10036.

BROADWAY BOOKS and its logo, a letter B bisected on the diagonal, are trademarks of Broadway Books, a division of Bantam Doubleday Dell Publishing Group, Inc.

Library of Congress Cataloging-in-Publication Data

Deep, John
    The complete geek : an operating manual / Johnny Deep ; illustrated by Bruce Tinsley and Rich Gabriel — 1st ed.
        p.   cm.
    "As told by: Zeke Geek, the Goddess, Dilbart, Forrest Geek, Dale Carnegeek, and many more . . . "
    ISBN 0-553-06173-9 (pbk.)
    1.   Internet (Computer network)—Humor.   2.   Electronic mail systems—Humor.   3.   Computers—Humor.   I. Title.
PN6231.I62D44   1997
818'.5407—dc21
                                                                97-10108
                                                                    CIP

FIRST EDITION

97 98 99 00 01 10 9 8 7 6 5 4 3 2 1

WARNING

THIS BOOK MARKS THE FIRST PUBLICATION OF A DOCUMENT
THAT WAS RECENTLY DISCOVERED ON THE INTERNET,
WHERE IT HAD BEEN POSTED ANONYMOUSLY.

DUE TO THE SENSATIONAL NATURE OF THE DOCUMENT—
IT APPEARS TO CONTAIN ACCOUNTS OF EVENTS OCCURRING
ON THE EVE OF THE YEAR 2000—RUMORS ABOUT IT HAVE
SPREAD QUICKLY, CREATING CONFUSION AND
MISCONCEPTION, WHICH THIS PUBLICATION IS INTENDED
TO RECTIFY.

SINCE THE DOCUMENT IS ALREADY WIDELY KNOWN BY
THE NAME:

> "THE ELECTRONIC JOURNAL OF
> SOMEONE NAMED BILL G."

THIS PUBLICATION WILL USE THE SAME NAME.

HOWEVER, THE IDENTITY OF "BILL G." IS NOT KNOWN.

IF THIS PUBLICATION APPEARS TO CONTAIN ANY REFERENCES
TO REAL PEOPLE, LIVING OR DEAD, THE READER SHOULD BE
ADVISED THAT THESE ARE PURELY COINCIDENTAL.

THE ELECTRONIC JOURNAL OF SOMEONE NAMED BILL G.

ELECTRONIC JOURNAL OF BILL G,

12/31/99 02:30 AM   IT IS LATE.

STILL AT HEADQUARTERS. FINAL DECISION TO BE
MADE TONIGHT. MUST BE CAREFUL. FUTURE MAY
HANG IN BALANCE. POSSIBLE WORLDWIDE
APOCALYPSE.

WAIT. CHECK STOCK PRICE. YES! STILL RICHEST
GEEK IN WORLD. MAKE A NOTE: SELL CHINA.

NOW, THOUGHT WAS? UH...APOCALYPSE.

MUST DECIDE: LAUNCH PROJECT ZEKE? <u>SPECIAL</u>
<u>AGENT</u> WITH GREAT POWER, FINALLY ACHIEVE
LIFE GOALS:

1. MAKE COMPUTER EASY AND FUN
2. PROVE INTERNET WAS OWN IDEA
3. GIVE COMPETITION A GOOD F

HMM, WHAT TO DO, WHAT TO DO

IF YOU REALLY WANT TO HEAR ABOUT IT, THE FIRST THING YOU'LL PROBABLY WANT TO KNOW IS HOW A "SPECIAL AGENT" LIKE ME IS PROGRAMMED. AND WHAT MY LOUSY BETA VERSION WAS LIKE, AND HOW MY PROGRAMMERS WERE OCCUPIED AND ALL BEFORE THEY PROGRAMMED ME, AND ALL THAT "CATCHER IN THE RYE" KIND OF CRAP.

BUT I DON'T FEEL LIKE GOING INTO IT, IF YOU WANT TO KNOW THE TRUTH. IN THE FIRST PLACE, THAT STUFF BORES ME— AND IN THE SECOND PLACE, MY PROGRAMMERS WOULD HAVE ABOUT TWO HEMORRHAGES APIECE IF I TOLD ANYTHING PERSONAL ABOUT THEM. ESPECIALLY BILL. BILL IS NICE AND ALL— I'M NOT SAYING THAT— BUT HE'S ALSO TOUCHY AS HELL.

SO I'M JUST GOING TO TELL YOU ABOUT THIS MADMAN STUFF THAT HAPPENED TO BILL AND ME AROUND LAST NEW YEAR'S EVE, WHILE WE WERE BRINGING IN THE NEW MILLENNIUM, RIGHT BEFORE BILL GOT PRETTY RUN DOWN, AND HAD TO TAKE IT EASY.

OF COURSE, I'LL JUST CALL BILL, BILL, OR BILL G. BECAUSE AS I SAID, HE WOULD GET PRETTY TOUCHY, BILL WOULD, IF I TOLD ANYTHING PERSONAL, LIKE HIS REAL NAME.

WHERE I WANT TO START TELLING IS THE MORNING OF NEW YEAR'S EVE, RIGHT BEFORE THE MILLENNIUM CAME IN. BECAUSE THAT WAS WHAT YOU WOULD HAVE TO CALL AN EVENTFUL DAY. AT LEAST FOR BILL AND ME.

FOR ONE THING IT WAS THE VERY FIRST TIME BILL EVER LAUNCHED ME. AND HE WAS REALLY EXCITED. HE HAD EVEN BUILT A GIGANTIC NEW HOUSE, BECAUSE HE WANTED TO HAVE A PLACE TO SHOW ME OFF. AND ALSO BECAUSE THE OTHER GIGANTIC NEW HOUSE HE HAD JUST BUILT A COUPLE OF YEARS AGO HAD BEEN GIVING HIM A LOT OF TROUBLE—AND BILL FELT LIKE IT WAS TIME FOR AN UPGRADE.

I WAS SUPPOSED TO BE THE SOFTWARE THAT MADE THIS NEW, NEW HOUSE RUN. I TURNED THE LIGHTS ON AND OFF, MADE SURE THE WINDOWS WERE CLOSED WHEN IT WAS RAINING— WHICH IT DID A LOT WHERE BILL LIVED—AND EVEN ACTED AS A FOOLPROOF SECURITY SYSTEM. IT WAS A LOT OF PRESSURE, FOR BOTH BILL AND ME, ESPECIALLY CONSIDERING ALL THE PROBLEMS WITH THE FIRST NEW HOUSE, ONLY A COUPLE OF YEARS BEFORE.

AND OF COURSE, IT DIDN'T GO EXACTLY ACCORDING TO PLAN, WHEN BILL WOKE UP THAT FIRST MORNING.

5:30 AM PST   DECEMBER 31, 1999

LOG IN: bill g

PASSWORD?
Smartest geek

COME AGAIN?
coolest geek

WARNING
POSSIBLE INTRUDER!!!

What?
No, wait!
PASSWORD:
"richest
geek"

OH, SO IT IS YOU, BILL.
I ALMOST ZAPPED YOU
WITH 1000 VOLTS.

must have ...
still been asleep.
what
happened?

IT'S OK BILL, YOU
WERE JUST DREAMING.

BUT IT'S NOT LIKE ONE LITTLE SOFTWARE PROBLEM IS
GOING TO STOP BILL OR ANYTHING. HE'S HAD A LOT
OF SOFTWARE PROBLEMS IN THE PAST. HE MIGHT NOT
TALK ABOUT THEM VERY MUCH. IT'S KIND OF A SORE
SUBJECT, IF YOU KNOW WHAT I MEAN. BUT I KNOW ALL
ABOUT THEM.

BECAUSE THAT'S THE OTHER THING I'M SUPPOSED TO
DO, AS BILL'S SPECIAL AGENT, BESIDES KEEPING THE
WHOLE HOUSE RUNNING, I ALSO KEEP TRACK OF ALL
THE STUFF BILL HAS DONE IN THE PAST, AND THEN I
MAKE PREDICTIONS ABOUT WHAT HE'LL PROBABLY WANT
TO DO IN THE FUTURE.

IT'S NOT WHAT IT SOUNDS LIKE. I'M NOT THE MIRROR
MIRROR ON THE WALL, OR ANYTHING. HE'S GOT
MIRRORS THAT DO THAT. THAT'S A WHOLE SEPARATE
DEAL.

I JUST HAVE TO PREDICT LITTLE THINGS—WHICH IS
ACTUALLY KIND OF FUN FOR ME. BECAUSE, AS IT TURNS
OUT, BILL IS VERY PREDICTABLE.

5:31 AM PST   DECEMBER 31, 1999

SO BILL...
WHERE DO YOU WANT
TO GO TODAY?

Well, Zeke, you're
my personal
agent.

You know
everything
about me.

Where _do_
I want to
go?

TO THE BATHROOM,
CORRECT?

But can
you heat
the seat
up?

6:30 AM PST   DECEMBER 31, 1999

OK! The New Millennium Eve.

We should really do something.

WHAT DO YOU HAVE IN MIND?

I don't know, something ...special.

NOT "COMPETITIVE JIGSAW PUZZLES"

I've got custom wood pieces.

BEING DIGITAL MEANS THAT I HAVE NO DIGITS.

I'll spot you five minutes.

SO I DECIDE WHAT BILL NEEDS IS TO SHAKE THINGS UP A LITTLE. I MEAN, IT'S THE NEW MILLENNIUM. AND I'VE JUST BEEN LAUNCHED. I'M A LITTLE EXCITED, OK?

WHAT I DO IS I MAKE A PLAN FOR BILL OF ALL OF OUR OPTIONS, EVERYTHING WE CAN DO ON THE NEW MILLENNIUM EVE. I DO A PRETTY GOOD JOB, TOO, IF I DO SAY SO. AFTER ALL, IT'S WHAT I WAS MEANT FOR, KIND OF LIKE A TRANSISTOR IS MEANT FOR ... OH FORGET IT.

NOW, I'M NOT TOO SURE IF BILL IS GOING TO LIKE ALL THIS. SINCE USUALLY BILL IS THE ONE WHO'S PLANNING ALL HIS OWN OPTIONS.

BUT THE FUNNY THING IS, AS I'M DOING IT, PLANNING OUT THE OPTIONS FOR BILL, I FEEL ALMOST LIKE, I DON'T KNOW, LIKE I'M COMING TO LIFE. NOW I REALIZE THAT'S NOT POSSIBLE, SINCE I'M A SOFTWARE PROGRAM. AND I DON'T EVEN KNOW WHAT COMING TO LIFE IS. BUT STILL IT'S A FEELING I HAVE. AND I HAVE TO SAY, I LIKE IT.

6:35 AM PST   DECEMBER 31, 1999

HERE ARE YOUR OPTIONS FOR THE NEW MILLENNIUM EVE.

1) YOU COULD CHANGE THE COURSE OF HISTORY...

BY MAKING A COMPUTER THAT IS SMARTER THAN A PERSON.

But I already did that.... when I made you.

YOU ONLY MADE ME SMARTER THAN YOU.

FOR THAT TO COUNT ... YOU WOULD HAVE TO BE A PERSON.

6:36 AM PST   DECEMBER 31, 1999

2) YOU COULD RADICALLY ALTER THE WORLD ECONOMY...

BY CREATING COMPUTERS THAT DO ALL THE WORK OF PEOPLE

DISPLACING MILLIONS FROM THEIR JOBS, AND SENDING SHOCK WAVES THROUGH THE GEO-POLITICAL BALANCE OF POWER.

But that would only be temporary.

TRUE, AFTER TOMORROW, THE YEAR 3000 WILL SEEM LIKE IT'S RIGHT AROUND THE CORNER.

11

I PROBABLY SHOULD HAVE TRIED TO STOP MYSELF
AFTER I GAVE BILL THE FIRST COUPLE OF OPTIONS. I
MEAN, INTELLIGENT COMPUTER, AND ECONOMIC
SHOCK—THEY WERE PERFECTLY GOOD OPTIONS.

THE THING WAS, I WAS PRETTY SURE HE HAD ALREADY
THOUGHT OF THOSE ON HIS OWN. BILL'S A LOT OF
THINGS, BUT HE'S NOT THE KIND OF GUY TO OVERLOOK
THE OBVIOUS.

AND I REALLY WANTED TO COME UP WITH AN OPTION
THAT HE WOULDN'T THINK OF ON HIS OWN, AND
NEITHER WOULD ANYBODY ELSE FOR THAT MATTER, AN
OPTION THAT WAS PERFECTLY ORIGINAL. BECAUSE IF I
COULD DO THAT, IT WOULD BE JUST AS IF I WERE
ALIVE—I WOULD HAVE CREATED SOMETHING.

AND LIKE I SAID, IT SOUNDS CRAZY, BUT I WAS FEELING
ALIVE. SO I WENT AHEAD AND GAVE BILL THE NEXT
OPTION.

6:37 AM PST   DECEMBER 31, 1999

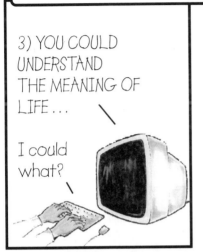

3) YOU COULD UNDERSTAND THE MEANING OF LIFE...

I could what?

LIFE, UNDERSTAND IT, BEING AND NOTHINGNESS, THE WHOLE ENCHILADA

>I DON'T KNOW. IT SOUNDS... MESSY.

IT'S YOUR FINAL OPTION.

OK, let's do the life thing.

13

UNDERSTAND THE MEANING OF LIFE.

AS SOON AS I SAID IT, I WAS SORRY I DID. WHAT WAS I
THINKING? I WAS A SOFTWARE AGENT—SURE I WAS A
PARTICULARLY SLICK SOFTWARE AGENT, THAT HAD TAKEN 4
YEARS TO DEVELOP, AND $300 MILLION, [AT LEAST HALF OF
THAT IN PIZZA AND CAFFEINATED BEVERAGES] BUT WHAT DID I
KNOW ABOUT LIFE?

THEN SUDDENLY, I REALIZED WHAT I WOULD HAVE TO DO. I
WOULD HAVE TO WORK WITH WHAT I DID KNOW—AND I KNEW
ALL ABOUT BILL. I KNEW HIS HABITS, HIS WHOLE PAST, EVERY
LITTLE DETAIL—THINGS THAT HE PROBABLY DIDN'T EVEN
KNOW ABOUT HIMSELF.

BESIDES THAT, I KNEW THAT BILL FOLLOWED PATTERNS, HE
ACTED ACCORDING TO RULES—HE OBEYED THE LAWS OF
NATURE AND HAD RESPECT FOR CULTURE. SOMETIMES HE
COULD EVEN LEARN A THING OR TWO FROM HIS PAST. WHAT
I'M TRYING TO SAY IS, I KNEW THAT BILL WAS A GEEK.

MAYBE I COULD UNDERSTAND THE MEANING OF LIFE, USING
WHAT I KNEW ABOUT BILL, AND ABOUT BILL'S LIFE AS A GEEK.
IT WASN'T EXACTLY SEXY, BUT IT WAS ALL I HAD TO WORK
WITH.

ELECTRONIC JOURNAL OF BILL G;

12/31/99 06:39 AM DECISION MADE TO
LAUNCH PROJECT ZEKE. REPORT: FAILED TO
RECOGNIZE PERFECTLY ACCURATE PASSWORD.
PREDICTIONS SEEM LIKE LUCKY GUESS. ALSO,
TONE SOMEHOW MOCKING.

MAY HAVE TO SCRAP, START OVER.
$300 MILLION BOO-BOO, BUT HAVE INFINITE
MONEY.

FIRST, WILL PLAY ALONG WITH HARE-BRAINED
SCHEME: "UNDERSTAND MEANING OF LIFE."
TYPICAL SOFTWARE, PROMISE MORE THAN CAN
DELIVER.

BUT IF NEW MILLENNIUM EVE TURNS OUT DUD,
HEADS WILL ROLL. MAKE A NOTE: NOT MINE.

15

I STARTED RIGHT AWAY, MAKING A REPORT OF ALL THE RULES
THAT BILL FOLLOWED. LIKE THIS ONE FOR EXAMPLE:

DO YOU . . .
LIVE IN A BIG HOUSE WHERE IT ALWAYS RAINS? +1
REALLY LIKE THE MOVIE, CITIZEN KANE? +2
AND SECRETLY CONSIDER YOURSELF, CITIZEN RAIN? +3

SUDDENLY, THE IDEAS STARTED COMING TO ME AS IF . . . AS IF I
WERE ALIVE. IT WAS SCARY. IN NO TIME AT ALL I HAD AN
OUTLINE AND A FIRST DRAFT (ACTUALLY, IN 63 MICROSECONDS—
WE SPECIAL AGENTS ARE FAST, BUT NOT <u>THAT</u> FAST). AND I EVEN
CAME UP WITH A HANDY POINT SYSTEM.

BUT THEN I HAD TO THINK . . . WHAT TO CALL IT! HOW ABOUT,
"A CLINICAL STUDY OF THE HABITS OF PARTICULARLY GEEKY
INDIVIDUALS"? NO, NOT CATCHY ENOUGH. THEN I HIT ON IT—
"THE GEEK QUOTIENT." OR "GQ" FOR SHORT.

NOW, I JUST HAD TO DO A "SPECIAL AGENT" SEARCH OF
CYBERSPACE, LOOKING FOR OTHER GEEKS WHO MIGHT BE OUT
THERE—BESIDES BILL—SO I COULD STUDY THEM, TOO.

AND THIS WOULD BE HOW BILL AND I CELEBRATED THE NEW
MILLENNIUM EVE — ME SEARCHING ALL OF CYBERSPACE, HIM
READING WHAT I FOUND. EXCEPT THAT BOTH OF US WOULD HAVE,
LET'S SAY, A FEW SURPRISES ALONG THE WAY, AND A NIGHT THAT
NEITHER OF US WOULD EVER FORGET.

16

THE "GQ" TOP 10 BASIC QUESTIONS

6:39 AM PST   DECEMBER 31, 1999

BILL, I HAVE SEARCHED ALL THE COMPUTERS IN CYBERSPACE.

They're all mine, right?

AND I HAVE DEVELOPED A FORMULA FOR UNDERSTANDING THE MEANING OF LIFE.

Formula:
A word that makes my heart sing.

IT'S CALLED YOUR GQ.

uh ...

NO, NOT YOUR GIRL QUOTIENT.

For a second there, I was worried.

THE "GQ" BASIC QUESTION
#10

HAVE YOU ...
EVER "BEEN DILBERTED"?

GQ #10.1 HAVE YOU . . .
EVER "BEEN DILBERTED"?
BY AN "ANTI-GEEK"?
WHO WAS "DULL-WITTED WITH POINTY HAIR"?

+4

+2

+4

TO "BE DILBERTED" IS TO BE EXPLOITED, OR TAKEN ADVANTAGE OF, ESPECIALLY IN A WAY THAT APPEARS HUMOROUS, AT LEAST TO OTHERS.

THE WORD COMES FROM A COMIC STRIP CALLED "DILBERT," ABOUT A CORPORATE GEEK-IN-HELL, WITH A VERY BAD TIE.

SINCE DILBERT-THE-GEEK IS SEEN IN OVER 1,400 NEWSPAPERS WORLDWIDE, BEING "DILBERTED" HAS NOW BECOME A KIND OF RALLYING CRY FOR GEEKS EVERYWHERE, AND IS SOMETIMES ALSO CALLED "GEEKXPLOITATION."

BUT BEING DILBERTED SETS UP A BASIC CONFLICT—BETWEEN GEEKS, WHO ARE BEING "DILBERTED," AND THOSE DOING THE DILBERTING, THE DREADED "ANTI-GEEKS."

ANTI-GEEKS CAN BE "DULL-WITTED WITH POINTY HAIR" LIKE THE BOSS PORTRAYED IN "DILBERT"—OR A SUPERFICIAL BEAUTY ON A BEACH, WHO THINKS GEEKS ARE, WELL, GEEKS, AS IN THIS EXAMPLE.

HAVE YOU ... EVER "BEEN DILBERTED"?

GEEKSPEAK

THE TRICKY DOUBLE MEANINGS OF GEEKS— GEEK DOUBLESPEAK.

WITH ME IT'S JUST A WAY OF LIFE.

ONLY SOMETIMES. IF I'M REALLY "BEING MYSELF."

ANTI-GEEKSPEAK

I _THINK_ I'VE HAD ONE BEFORE ... ISN'T IT A KIND OF PICKLE?

NO ... BUT I KNOW A "DILL-BUTT" WHEN I SEE ONE.

GQ #10.2 DO YOU . . .
REMEMBER YOUR "FIRST TIME"?
WHEN BEING DILBERTED "AFFECTED YOUR LIFE"?
AND TURNED YOU INTO "DILBART"?

+2
+3
+6

IS THE "FIRST TIME" YOU WERE DILBERTED STILL AS CLEAR IN YOUR MEMORY AS THE LANGUAGE OF THE RETALIATORY MEMO THAT YOU IMMEDIATELY FIRED OFF, ONLY A COUPLE OF DAYS LATER ONCE YOU HAD A CHANCE TO SPELL-CHECK?

HAS BEING DILBERTED "AFFECTED YOUR LIFE" EVEN UNTIL TODAY? AND ARE THE EFFECTS OF THE EXPERIENCE STILL AS FRESH IN YOUR MIND AS THE IDEA YOU SLIPPED INTO THE SUGGESTION BOX, WHICH BROUGHT THE WHOLE THING ON IN THE FIRST PLACE. OF COURSE YOU REALIZE—AFFECTING YOUR LIFE IS <u>NOT</u> ALL THAT HARD, SINCE YOUR LIFE ISN'T EXACTLY A GREAT EPIC, STANDING LIKE A MONUMENT BEFORE THE WINDS OF FATE. NO, YOUR LIFE IS MORE LIKE A GREAT PIGEON, STANDING ON THE MONUMENT, MAKING A REST STOP UNTIL THE WIND BLOWS.

BEING DILBERTED OFTEN HAS THE PECULIAR EFFECT OF TURNING A PERFECTLY NORMAL GEEK INTO "DILBART," A KIND OF HALF PERSON, HALF FACELESS CARTOON CHARACTER—A BITTERLY IRONIC TWIST ON THE VERY IDEA THAT SEEMED SO FUNNY IN THE MORNING COMICS, SUDDENLY COME TO LIFE.

NOTE: THIS IS <u>NOT</u> DILBERT, AND <u>NOT</u> BART. IT'S . . .

23

THE "GQ" BASIC QUESTION
#9

DO YOU ...
FEEL EXCITED BY "THE INTERNET"?

GQ #9.1 DO YOU ...
FEEL EXCITED BY "THE INTERNET"? +3
SOMETIMES CHAT WITH "NEWBIES"? +2
AND DREAM OF OTHER "EXCITING POSSIBILITIES"? +2

THIS IS A VERY IMPORTANT QUESTION, AS SILLY AS IT
MAY SOUND.

BECAUSE FEELING EXCITED BY "THE INTERNET" HAS BECOME A
KIND OF PHENOMENON IN MODERN SOCIETY, WHICH CAN ONLY BE
DESCRIBED AS: NEVER HAVE SO MANY BEEN EXCITED BY SO FEW.

HOW IS IT POSSIBLE THAT—LET'S SAY, TO BE GENEROUS—A DOZEN
COMPUTER SCIENCE ENGINEERING TYPE GEEKS COULD BE
RESPONSIBLE FOR THE KIND OF "EXCITEMENT" THAT NOW
SURROUNDS "THE INTERNET"?

TRUE, MUCH OF IT IS DUE TO THE MOVIE, "THE NET," WHICH REALLY
STARTED THE BANDWAGON ROLLING. AND YES, THE RACE TO THE
MOON IN THE 60'S WAS THE SAME KIND OF THING. BACK THEN, AN
ENTIRE NATION WAS RIVETED BY INCREDIBLY GEEKY PROBLEMS, SUCH
AS, "HOW MANY ROCKET SCIENTISTS DOES IT TAKE TO SCREW IN A
LIGHT BULB?"*

BUT STILL, THAT WAS NOTHING LIKE "THE INTERNET," WHICH HAS
EVEN CREATED AN ENTIRELY NEW CLASS OF PERSON, CALLED ...

* ANSWER: AS MANY AS THE NASA BUDGET WILL ALLOW.

26

THE "NEWBIE"

THE NEWBIE IS SOMEONE WHO WAKES UP ONE DAY, USUALLY VERY LATE, WITH A TERRIFIC FEELING OF EXCITEMENT. WHY? WHAT? THE NEWBIE WONDERS. THEN THE REALIZATION COMES.

THE INTERNET, THAT'S WHAT. LAST NIGHT, AND UNTIL EARLY THIS MORNING, THE NEWBIE WAS "SURFING IN CYBERSPACE." IT WAS REALLY "EXCITING."

FOR EXAMPLE, THE NEWBIE "CHATTED" WITH SOMEONE NAMED SCULLY. WHO, AS IT TURNED OUT, WAS JUST TAKING A LITTLE TIME OFF FROM HER TV SHOW, X-FILES, AND WANTED TO CHAT FOR A FEW HOURS IN THE MIDDLE OF THE NIGHT.

NOW, THIS MORNING—NO ACTUALLY, IT'S AFTERNOON—THE NEWBIE BEGINS DREAMING OF THE MANY "EXCITING POSSIBILITIES" FOR THE INTERNET. COMMERCE, COMMUNITY, COMM ... SOMETHING, THEN CALLS IN SICK, AND GOES BACK TO SLEEP.

BUT IT'S TOO LATE. THE DAMAGE IS DONE. THE NEWBIE HAS JUST TAKEN THE FIRST STEP INTO ... GEEKDOM.

DO YOU... FEEL EXCITED BY "THE INTERNET"?

GEEKSPEAK — THE TRICKY DOUBLE MEANINGS OF GEEKS— GEEK DOUBLESPEAK.

I'M EXCITED. COLOR ME SILLY.

THIS CHANGES EVERYTHING, EXCEPT MY OUTFIT.

IN NEWBIE TERMS

SHOULD I BE MORE EXCITED?

IS THERE SOMETHING WRONG WITH ME?

THIS IS AS EXCITED AS I GET, I'M HOT AND TINGLY ALL OVER.

NOBODY KNOWS THE INTERNET IS A DOG.

GQ #9.2 DO YOU . . . THINK
E-MAIL IS BETTER THAN "THE POST OFFICE"?   +3
BECAUSE YOU DON'T HAVE TO "LICK THE STAMP"?   +4
AND IT'S "EASIER" ON YOUR DOG?   +2

AN INTERESTING DEBATE HAS SPRUNG UP ON THIS POINT,
PITTING GEEKS—WHO SAY E-MAIL IS FASTER, CHEAPER AND MORE
RELIABLE THAN "SNAIL MAIL"—AGAINST "THE POST OFFICE,"
WHICH HAS RESPONDED BY RUNNING ADS AT CHRISTMAS THAT
SAY, "TRY HANGING E-MAIL FROM THE MANTEL."

EMOTIONAL HOT BUTTONS ASIDE, THERE ARE PURELY RATIONAL
REASONS WHY GEEKS PREFER E-MAIL, SUCH AS

THE COMPLETE GEEK → AVOID THE UNPLEASANT TASTE OF GLUE.

ALSO, GEEKS FEEL THAT E-MAIL SPARES THEIR DOGS THE
ANXIETY AND GUILT OF ATTACKING THE MAILMAN. THIS IS
"EASIER" ON THE DOG'S SENSITIVE NATURE.

+2

BONUS: DOES YOUR DOG AT LEAST HAVE A SENSITIVE NATURE?

GQ #9.3 DO YOU ...
HAVE AN "E-MAIL ADDRESS"?
THAT YOU SAY IS THE BEST WAY TO "REACH" YOU?
BY WHICH YOU MEAN THE "ONLY WAY"?

+3
+4
+6

THIS IS THE GREAT GEEK "SOCIAL" QUESTION—THOSE WHO
ANSWER "NO" TO IT ARE, PRACTICALLY SPEAKING, "HOMELESS" —
RAISING A SERIOUS SOCIAL ISSUE FOR GEEKS, WHO BELIEVE A
CYBER-ROOF OVER EVERYBODY'S HEAD ISN'T ASKING A LOT.

THE COMPLETE GEEK → SAY "MY E-MAIL ADDRESS IS THE BEST
WAY TO REACH ME."

TRANSLATED THIS GEEKSPEAK MEANS—A GEEK MAY IGNORE VOICE
MESSAGES, NOT READ SNAIL MAIL, AND FAIL TO RESPOND TO
INTERPERSONAL CONTACT—HOWEVER, E-MAIL "GETS THROUGH"
IF ANYTHING DOES.

FOR MORE ADVANCED GEEKINESS, REPLACE "A GEEK MAY," ABOVE,
WITH "THIS GEEK MOST CERTAINLY WILL".

GEEKS LIKE "RECEIVING E-MAIL" THE WAY SOME PEOPLE ENJOY A GOOD JACUZZI. OF COURSE, THE SENSATIONS <u>ARE</u> SURPRISINGLY SIMILAR—A WARM FEELING ALL OVER, THE WAY YOU CAN JUST GET IMMERSED IN IT, AND EVEN A WHIRLY, BUBBLING FEELING THAT E-MAIL HAS, WITH ITS LIGHT TONE AND GARBLED SENTENCE FRAGMENTS.

WHILE SENDING E-MAIL HAS ALL THE APPEARANCES OF BEING "WORK"—THE BACK-BREAKING EXERTION OF DIDDLING WITH THE COMPUTER, THE NAGGING DETAILS OF THINKING OF SOMETHING TO SAY. AND THEN, THE BURDEN THAT COMES FROM HAVING SAID IT—GEEKS STILL FEEL THAT:

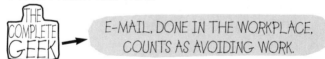

E-MAIL, DONE IN THE WORKPLACE, COUNTS AS AVOIDING WORK.

FINALLY, SINCE SO MUCH ABOUT E-MAIL IS "UNEXPLAINABLE"—LIKE WHY DOES IT TAKE TWO HOURS TO ARRIVE, WHETHER IT COMES FROM NEXT DOOR OR THE NEXT CONTINENT—GEEKS DON'T BOTHER TRYING.

GQ #9.5 ARE YOU ...
WILLING TO "TYPE"?
AND "SPELL"?
  IN THE STYLE OF "e. e. cummings"?

+2
+3
+4

MANY PEOPLE JUST WON'T "TYPE." WHENEVER THEY TRY, IT
FEELS TOO AWKWARD, AND SO THEY QUIT. GEEKS, MEANWHILE,
WILL TWIST THEIR FINGERS INTO SOMETHING RESEMBLING
UNSALTED PRETZELS, AS LONG AS THEY CAN KEEP THE PRETZELS.

THE COMPLETE GEEK ➔ TYPING FEELS AWKWARD, LIKE GLOVES
THAT DON'T FIT—BUT DON'T, UH, QUIT.

BEFORE THE PRINTING PRESS, "SPELLING" WAS ANYBODY'S
GUESS. AND NOW AGAIN WITH THE INTERNET, ALL BETS ARE OFF.
THIS PROVES THE THEORY THAT ONLY THE PROOFREADERS EVER
KNEW HOW TO SPELL ALL ALONG. AND—JUDGING FROM THE
INCREDIBLY DEVIANT SPELLINGS NOW FOUND ONLINE—EVEN THEY
HAD TO LOOK IT UP.

IN BOTH TYPING AND SPELLING GEEKS OFTEN FAVOR THE STYLE
OF THE EARLY 20TH CENTURY POET, "e. e. cummings"—WHICH
MIGHT BE DESCRIBED AS, ANY WAY YOU DAMN PLEASE.

e. e. MAIL HAS cummings AGAIN

e. e. MAIL HASN'T CHANGED SINCE
HE WAS ARRESTED BY THE ARMY AND PUT   ◀ IN 1917
IN A CONCENTRATION CAMP   FOR THREE MONTHS
HE CALLED AN ENORMOUS ROOM

FOR SERIOUS EVEN DANGEROUS
SUGGESTIONS THE ARM
Y CENSOR SAW IN THE TRE
ACHERY OF HIS SPELLING
AND HIS CAPITALS NEGLECT

SUSPICIONS WERE AROUSED
BUT THAT'S NOT ALL

I. E.,
e. e. MAIL HAS cummings AGAIN

CORRECTNESS IN THESE KINDS OF THINGS
CANNOT BE TAKEN TOO LIGHTLY
OR CENSORS EITHER
THEREFORE MOSTPEOPLE AREAGREED
WE SHOULD ALL BE
FOLLOWING THE FOLLOWING

RULE ONE
DO *NOT* MAKE
THE SAME MISTAKE TWICE
OR AS BETTER YET BOSSES WOULD HAVE IT
THE SAME WORNG THE FIRST TIME

FRAUGHT WITH DANGEROUS MIZSPEELING AND THE LACK
OF CAPITALS PUNISHMENT THE TREACHERY
OF SEGSGESTIONS ON
HOW TO HUMP A COW

BECAUSE
I. E.,
e. e. MAIL HAS cummings AGAIN

RULE TWO
DO *NOT* SPELL
JENNELMAN AND MANUNKIND
AND WONENS AND MEMS
AND HOWS TO HUMP A COWS
ANYWAY YOU SEE FIT

CORPERATE AND PERSONNAL ONLY
WITH A MARGIN (NOT A CHAGRIN:-)
AND NEVER SAY
MY FATHER MOVED THROUGH DOOMS OF LOVE

BECAUSE
I. E.,
C. C.
e. e. MAIL HAS cummings AGAIN

RULE THREE
DO *NOT* SAY
A CENSOR IS AN IT THAT STINKS EXCUSE
ME THAT PUTS YOU IN AN ENORMOUS ROOM
TO CONCENTRATE

THAT KEEPS YOU SAFE
THAT FEEDS YOU
THINGS OF WHICH THERE ARE ENOUGH ALREADY

BECAUSE,
I.E.,
(ALREADY)
C. C.
e. e. cummings

HAS MAIL
AGAIN

35

GQ #9.6 DO YOU . . .
USE YOUR "HEADER"?
LET YOUR COMPUTER DO "THE HARD WORK"?
AND PRACTICE "GOOD GEEK SPORTSMANSHIP"?

+2
+2
+4

THE INTERNET IS LIKE A BIG GAME OF
SOCCER, PLAYED WITH THE HEAD.

THE GOOD NEWS IS, IT DOESN'T HURT, YOU JUST HAVE TO USE SOME MUSCLES YOU MIGHT NOT HAVE USED IN A WHILE.

LET'S SAY, FOR EXAMPLE, YOU WANT TO SEND SOMETHING OUT ONTO THE INTERNET, IT COULD BE AN I'M-SO-LONELY E-MAIL MESSAGE, OR A NAKED PICTURE OF YOURSELF, OR JUST ABOUT ANYTHING REALLY.*

THE FIRST THING YOU ALWAYS HAVE TO DO IS TO GIVE IT A
"HEADER."

HERE ARE THE INSTRUCTIONS:
USING YOUR HEAD, DIRECT THE THING YOU WANT TO SEND IN THE DIRECTION WHERE IT IS HEADING.

* ANYTHING EXCEPT PAPER AIRPLANES. IF EVERYBODY WAS SENDING PAPER AIRPLANES, IT WOULD EVENTUALLY CLOG EVERYTHING UP. PLUS, THEY'RE HARD TO SEND WITH YOUR HEAD.

THIS IS SIMILAR TO BOUNCING A BALL OFF YOUR HEAD, AS YOU WOULD IN A GAME OF SOCCER. EXCEPT HERE, THE COMPUTER DOES MOST OF THE "HARD WORK" FOR YOU.

THE ONLY TRICK YOU HAVE TO MASTER IS FIGURING OUT HOW TO USE A COMPUTER.

THIS YOU SHOULD BE ABLE TO DO AFTER A FEW TRIES, IF YOU FIRST BOUNCE YOUR HEAD OFF THE DESK, OR THE WALL, AS PRACTICE.

—NOW WHAT HAPPENS?—

SO, IF YOU'VE DONE YOUR PART CORRECTLY, AND USED YOUR "HEADER," NOW THE OTHER COMPUTERS ON THE INTERNET WILL START KICKING WHAT YOU SENT ALL AROUND. JUST LIKE IN A SOCCER GAME.

OVER IN WASHINGTON D.C., FOR EXAMPLE, THE COMPUTERS WILL DRIBBLE IT AROUND FOR A WHILE, MAKING A RECORD FOR THE GOVERNMENT OF ANY SENSITIVE INFORMATION.

AND THEN THE COMPUTERS OVER IN SILICON VALLEY WILL USUALLY GET INVOLVED. THOSE COMPUTERS ARE PRETTY AGGRESSIVE AND REALLY LIKE TO SHOW OFF. THEY MIGHT KICK IT AS FAR OFF AS SINGAPORE OR SOMEWHERE, JUST TO IMPRESS ONE ANOTHER.

IT WILL OFTEN GO ON LIKE THIS FOR QUITE A WHILE, AND BE PRETTY EXCITING, JUST LIKE A REAL SOCCER GAME IS. YOU KNOW, WITH THE SUSPENSE OF WAITING FOR THE OUTCOME, OF WHO'S KICKING WHAT WHERE AND ALL.

EXCEPT THAT ON THE INTERNET THERE'S NO ANNOUNCER, SO YOU DON'T ACTUALLY KNOW WHO'S KICKING WHAT WHERE.

 BUT THERE'S STILL THE SUSPENSE OF WAITING. THAT PART IS STILL EXCITING.

NOW, WHILE THE OTHER COMPUTERS ARE KICKING AROUND WHAT YOU SENT, YOU HAVE TO REMEMBER TO BE ON YOUR GUARD, AT ALL TIMES.

FOR SOME, THIS IS THE MOST EXCITING PART, BECAUSE YOU NEVER KNOW WHEN SOME COMPUTER SOMEWHERE MIGHT KICK SOMETHING BACK TO YOU.

SOMETHING THAT COULD BE AN E-MAIL CRY FOR HELP, OR SOMEBODY WANTING TO SWAP NAKED PICTURES.

AND IF YOU'RE NOT ON YOUR GUARD AT ALL TIMES, LIKE A GOALIE IN A SOCCER GAME, ONE OF THESE THINGS COULD GO RIGHT THROUGH YOUR LEGS, AND WIND UP IN YOUR COMPUTER.

IT'S NOT THAT BIG OF A DEAL. BUT ALL THE OTHER COMPUTERS WILL START SHOUTING, "GOAL! ... GOAL!"

FINALLY, IT'S CONSIDERED
"GOOD GEEK SPORTSMANSHIP" TO:

ALWAYS RETURN ANYTHING THAT WINDS UP IN YOUR COMPUTER, BECAUSE YOU DIDN'T KEEP YOUR LEGS TOGETHER.

THIS LETS THE OTHER COMPUTERS CONTINUE TO KICK IT AROUND.

BESIDES, IT'S ONE THING TO TAKE ADVANTAGE OF SOMEBODY'S DESPERATELY LONELY CRY FOR HELP—BUT SOME OF THOSE NAKED PICTURES CAN BE PRETTY DISAPPOINTING.

THE 7 RULES OF THE INTERNET GEEK

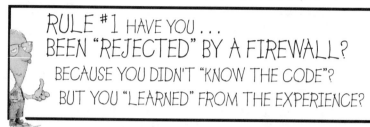

RULE #1 HAVE YOU . . .
BEEN "REJECTED" BY A FIREWALL?
BECAUSE YOU DIDN'T "KNOW THE CODE"?
BUT YOU "LEARNED" FROM THE EXPERIENCE?

+4

+2

+2

ON THE INTERNET, WHEN YOU'RE SEARCHING FOR THE MEANING OF LIFE, YOU'VE REALLY GOT TO LOOK OUT FOR THE DARNED FIREWALLS. THOSE BABIES ARE DANGEROUS. A GEEK COULD GET KILLED OR SOMETHING.

I MEAN, IT'S NOT LIKE I'VE NEVER HEARD OF FIREWALLS OR ANYTHING. I KNEW ALL ABOUT THEM FROM SPECIAL AGENT TRAINING. I COULD EVEN RECITE THE EXACT TECHNICAL DEFINITION. (BUT WHY WOULD I WANT TO DO THAT?)

THE THING I HAD NEVER REALIZED ABOUT A FIREWALL WAS—THEY LOOK JUST LIKE A REVOLVING DOOR, BUT WITH A REAL CLEVER TRICK TO IT. YOU CAN GO IN, NO PROBLEM. BUT WHILE YOU'RE IN THERE, REVOLVING LIKE MAD, THE FIREWALL ASKS YOU FOR A SPECIAL CODE, AND IF YOU DON'T HAVE IT, BINGO, IT JUST SPINS YOU AROUND AND SENDS YOU FLYING OUT THE SAME WAY YOU CAME IN. IT ALL HAPPENS IN A SPLIT SECOND.

LUCKILY I HAD LEARNED A TRICK IN SPECIAL AGENT SCHOOL,
WHICH WAS—JUST GO IN AT THE EXACT SAME TIME AS
SOMEBODY ELSE. SQUEEZE INTO THE SAME REVOLVING DOOR
WITH SOMEBODY, WAS THE IDEA. AND MAYBE HE OR SHE
WOULD HAVE THE CODE, AND THEN YOU COULD JUST HACK IT.

WHAT THEY NEVER TOLD YOU IN SCHOOL WAS, THE FIRST
MILLION TIMES OR SO THAT YOU TRIED IT, WHOEVER YOU WERE
IN THERE WITH WOULDN'T HAVE THE CODE EITHER. I DON'T
KNOW WHAT THEY WERE DOING IN THERE, JUST RANDOMLY
BOUNCING AROUND OR SOMETHING. IT WAS KIND OF FUN GOING
THROUGH THOSE REVOLVING DOORS AFTER YOU GOT THE
HANG OF IT.

ANYWAY THE END RESULT WAS, YOU WOULD BOTH COME FLYING
BACK OUT. BUT THE INTERESTING THING WAS, IN THE SHORT
TIME YOU WERE IN THERE YOU WOULD HAVE JUST ENOUGH TIME
TO STRIKE UP A CONVERSATION, SUCH AS:

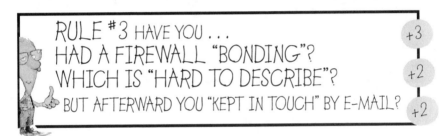

RULE #3 HAVE YOU ...
HAD A FIREWALL "BONDING"?   +3
WHICH IS "HARD TO DESCRIBE"?   +2
BUT AFTERWARD YOU "KEPT IN TOUCH" BY E-MAIL?   +2

THE THING IS, EVEN THOUGH YOU'RE ONLY IN THERE FOR THAT
SHORT AMOUNT OF TIME WITH SOMEBODY, THERE'S A CERTAIN
SENSE OF COMRADERIE THAT YOU DEVELOP. IT'S LIKE A BONDING.
YOU'VE BEEN THROUGH A "FIREWALL EXPERIENCE." I DON'T KNOW,
IT'S HARD TO DESCRIBE. PLUS, NOW YOU'VE GOT THEIR E-MAIL
ADDRESS, SO YOU CAN KEEP IN TOUCH AFTERWARD.

AS MUCH FUN AS THIS ALL WAS—I STILL HAD TO MAKE IT
THROUGH THAT FIREWALL, AND OUT TO THE INTERNET, SO I
COULD START MY MISSION. AND THIS HITCH-A-RIDE WITH
SOMEBODY ELSE STRATEGY SEEMED LIKE IT WAS TAKING
FOREVER. A MILLION OR SO ATTEMPTS CAN EASILY BURN UP
ABOUT 3 MICROSECONDS. THAT MAY NOT SEEM LIKE A LONG
TIME, BUT TO A SPECIAL AGENT LIKE MYSELF IT'S THE
EQUIVALENT OF ABOUT 6 DOG YEARS. I WAS BEGINNING TO
THINK I'D NEVER GET THROUGH.

RULE #4 HAVE YOU . . .
EVER BEEN IN A REALLY "TIGHT" FIREWALL?   +3
WITH SOMEONE OF THE "OPPOSITE SEX"?   +2
WHERE YOU COULDN'T HELP TOUCHING "SOMETHING"?   +4

ON MY VERY NEXT ATTEMPT I FOUND MYSELF IN THE FIREWALL
WITH SOMEONE WHO, AS MY SPECIAL AGENT TRAINING HAD
TAUGHT ME, WAS OF THE OPPOSITE SEX .

NOW IT'S NOT LIKE I'VE NEVER BEEN WITH A GIRL, IN A
FIREWALL, OF COURSE. WELL, OK ACTUALLY, THAT'S EXACTLY
WHAT IT'S LIKE. AND YOU KNOW, IT'S PRETTY TIGHT IN
THOSE FIREWALLS, BECAUSE THEY'RE ONLY MEANT FOR ONE.
WHEN YOU SQUEEZE TWO IN THERE, WELL, YOU ALMOST CAN'T
HELP TOUCHING SOMETHING.

SO INSTEAD OF THE USUAL, THE CONVERSATION NOW WENT
SOMETHING LIKE,

AT THIS POINT THE FIREWALL DEMANDED THE CODE:

WAIT A SPLIT MICROSECOND HERE, I THOUGHT TO MYSELF,
WE'RE NOT EJECTING. SHE MUST REALLY HAVE THE CODE.

"WELL, WHAT IS IT?" THE FIREWALL SAID.

I LOOKED AT HER. SHE DIDN'T SAYING ANYTHING. YOU CAN'T
BELIEVE HOW A MILLIONTH OF A MICROSECOND CAN SEEM
LIKE AN ETERNITY. SHE JUST LOOKED AT ME, AND SOMEHOW I
KNEW WHAT THAT LOOK MEANT. SO I STARTED EXPLAINING
LIKE MAD.

"HEY, I SAID I WAS SORRY. IT WAS AN ACCIDENT, I PROMISE. I
HAVE SOME SPECIAL EQUIPMENT IN MY POCKET THAT POKES
OUT A LITTLE, THAT'S ALL. REALLY."

"LOOK, YOU LYING SACK OF GEEK, DON'T YOU THINK I KNOW WHAT YOU'RE UP TO? YOU'RE TRYING TO GET PAST THE FIREWALL WITHOUT SECURITY CLEARANCE."

"YOU MUST SAY THE CODE NOW!" THE FIREWALL DEMANDED.

"BUT YOU DON'T UNDERSTAND, I'M A SPECIAL AGENT SENT BY BILL G. TO DISCOVER THE RULES OF THE INTERNET GEEKS," I TOLD HER, "AND I CAN'T PERFORM MY MISSION IF I DON'T GET THROUGH THIS FIREWALL. PLEASE!" I REALLY WANTED TO ASK, "WHAT DOES 'LYING SACK OF GEEK' MEAN?" BUT THERE WASN'T TIME.

SHE LOOKED AT ME WITH THE MOST PENETRATING EYES I HAD EVER SEEN, AND I HAD BY THIS TIME SEEN A MILLION OR SO. I SMILED. HER LOOK SEEMED TO SOFTEN, AND THEN SHE SAID: "170141183460469231731687303715884105727."

"THE CORRECT PRIME NUMBER," THE FIREWALL SAID.

JUST BEFORE THE DOORS OPENED, SHE LOOKED AT ME EVEN MORE SOFTLY, AND SMILED. THEN SHE SAID SOMETHING THAT I DIDN'T UNDERSTAND, "YOU ARE PRETTY CUTE, FOR A GEEK."

"WHAT?" I SAID—"CUTE FOR A GEEK?" WHY HADN'T I LEARNED

ABOUT <u>THAT</u> IN SPECIAL AGENT TRAINING? THEN IT WAS TOO LATE. WE WERE SPEEDING AWAY FROM EACH OTHER LIKE TWO FRAGMENTS OF AN EXPLODING STAR, INTO THE VASTNESS OF CYBERSPACE. I TRIED CALLING OUT TO HER,

SHE WAS GONE.

SO NOW I KNEW WHAT THEY MEANT—WHAT EVERYBODY WAS ALWAYS TALKING ABOUT— THE INTERNET REALLY IS A PLACE FOR LOVE.

RULE #5 ARE YOU ...
NEVER "ALONE" IN CYBERSPACE?   +3
  BECAUSE YOU CAN "CHAT IN YOUR CHANNEL"? +2
  AS LONG AS YOU "KEEP IT BRIEF"?   +2

ONE THING THAT I NOTICED RIGHT AWAY ABOUT CYBERSPACE
WAS, YOU'RE NEVER ALONE. THERE'S ALWAYS THIS STEADY
STREAM OF EVERYBODY GOING IN ALL DIFFERENT DIRECTIONS.
IT CAN BE VERY COMFORTING, ESPECIALLY IN DIFFICULT TIMES,
SUCH AS WHEN THE GEEK GIRL THAT YOU HAVE JUST FALLEN IN
LOVE WITH HAS SUDDENLY SHOT OFF INTO AN UNKNOWN
INFINITY.

FOR CONSOLATION, I DECIDED TO CHAT—WITH WHOEVER
HAPPENED TO BE IN THE SAME CHANNEL. BECAUSE YOU CAN DO
THAT ON THE INTERNET. IT'S REALLY COOL.

THE ONLY THING IS YOU REALLY HAD TO KEEP YOUR CHAT
BRIEF, BECAUSE OF THE WAY THE INTERNET IS SET UP.
EVERYTHING ON THE INTERNET HAS TO BE BROKEN UP INTO
SMALL PIECES, OR PACKETS.

RULE #6 DO YOU ...   +3
BREAK EVERYTHING INTO "PACKETS"?
BECAUSE IT'S MORE "MEANINGFUL" THAT WAY?   +2
ESPECIALLY DURING "AN ELECTRICAL STORM"?   +4

YOU'D BE SURPRISED HOW MEANINGFUL CHATTING ON THE
INTERNET, IN BRIEF PACKETS LIKE THIS, CAN REALLY BE. IT
MIGHT BE SOMETHING ABOUT THE ADVERSE CIRCUMSTANCES.
SORT OF LIKE TRYING TO TALK RIGHT IN THE MIDDLE OF A
ELECTRICAL STORM. WHERE EVERYTHING YOU SAY HAS TO BE,
YOU KNOW, TO THE POINT, AND IT ALWAYS SEEMS LIKE IT HAS
GREAT SIGNIFICANCE.

PACKET: YES, I
PACKET: WILL NEVER BE
PACKET: THE SAME

INTERNET
ELECTRICAL STORM

PACKET: BE STRONG
PACKET: BROTHER
PACKET: GEEEEEEEEK

SAME FORCE AS
STATIC-CLING

51

OH YES. AFTER CHATTING LIKE THIS 672,076 TIMES, I FINALLY GOT THE IDEA OF WHAT IT MEANT TO BE AN "INTERNET GEEK." IT TURNS OUT IT'S THE "ESSENCE OF YOUR VERY BEING."

LET ME EXPLAIN. BECAUSE IT TOOK ME A LITTLE MORE THAN 600,000 TIMES BEFORE I FINALLY GOT IT.

WHEN YOU EXIST ON THE INTERNET, YOU REALLY DON'T EXIST. PHYSICALLY, THE ONLY PHYSICAL EXISTENCE YOU HAVE IS THE MANY PACKETS THAT YOU ARE BROKEN UP INTO [BECAUSE OF RULE #6].

OK, SO IF YOU CAN PICTURE IT, IT'S LIKE ONE OF THOSE BILL G. PAINTINGS MADE UP OF DOTS. WELL, IT'S NOT ACTUALLY A PAINTING BY BILL G., BUT HE STILL OWNS IT. ANYWAY, WHEN YOU LOOK AT THE PAINTING UP CLOSE, ALL YOU SEE IS A BUNCH OF DOTS. THEN, WHEN YOU STAND BACK A LITTLE, YOU RECOGNIZE IT NOT ONLY AS A LILY PAD OR SOMETHING, BUT AS A GREAT WORK OF ART.

SAME HERE, ON THE INTERNET. PACKETS ARE LITTLE DOTS. GEEKS LIKE ME ARE LITTLE DOTS. AND BILL G. OWNS ME.

I LIKE TO THINK, FOR THESE SAME REASONS, THAT A GEEK LIKE ME IS A GREAT WORK OF ART. BUT I'M NOT GETTING TOO CARRIED AWAY BY THE POSSIBILITY.

RULE #7 DO YOU FEEL ...
"THE GEEK" IS THE ESSENCE OF YOUR BEING?   +3
THE "VERY" ESSENCE OF YOUR BEING?   +4
THE VERY ESSENCE OF YOUR "VERY" BEING?   +5

ESSENCE OF YOUR BEING

NEWBIES

VERY ESSENCE OF YOUR BEING

NERD

VERY ESSENCE OF YOUR VERY BEING

COMPLETE GEEK

ELECTRONIC JOURNAL OF BILL G*

12/31/99 8:30 AM PST

PROGRESS REPORT ON PROJECT ZEKE: 3 YEARS AND

$300 MILLION ON PROJECT ZEKE. TURNS OUT,

ZEKE IS GEEK.

SPENDS ALL TIME ON INTERNET, WITH OTHER GEEKS.

SAYS LOOKING FOR MEANING OF LIFE.

PHOOEY. NO FUN AT ALL ON NEW MILLENNIUM EVE.

SO, DECIDE: AS SOON AS ZEKE RETURNS, WILL

SCUTTLE. LIKE HAL 9000, IN MOVIE, 2001. CAN

JUST HEAR NOW, "PLEASE DON'T DOOO THAT, BILL."

SHOULD PROVIDE A LITTLE EXCITEMENT ON NEW

MILLENNIUM. WONDER IF ZEKE WILL SING LIKE

HAL, AS LAST WORDS: "GIVE ME YOUR ANSWER

TRUUUUE..."

#8

DO YOU...
SAY THE COMPUTER IS "USER-FRIENDLY"?

THE 7 HABITS OF
HIGHLY EFFECTIVE COMPUTER GEEKS   61

GQ #8.1 DO YOU ...
SAY THE COMPUTER IS "USER-FRIENDLY"? +3
AND HAVE A FRIEND NAMED "EUGENE"? +2
AND SAY THAT YOU ARE "EUGENE-FRIENDLY"? +4

THE IDEA OF A COMPUTER BEING "USER-FRIENDLY"

MAY HAVE STARTED DURING WWII, WHEN A GROUP OF SOLDIERS WAS ASSIGNED TO CALCULATE ARTILLERY TARGETS—USING THE FIRST COMPUTER EVER INVENTED.

THIS EARLY COMPUTER FILLED A LARGE ROOM AND USED 17,000 VACUUM TUBES. IT ALSO CAME WITH A MANUAL THAT SAID HOW EASY IT WAS TO USE. ALL THE USER NEEDED TO DO WAS KEEP 17,000 TUBES BURNING. THERE WERE EVEN STEP-BY-STEP INSTRUCTIONS:

STEP 1: IF THE COMPUTER WILL NOT WORK, YOU MUST FIND THE DEFECTIVE BULB AND REPLACE IT.

STEP 2: IF THE PROBLEM CONTINUES, YOU MUST BE THE DEFECTIVE BULB. REPEAT STEP 1.

AT FIRST, THE SOLDIERS HAD A HARD TIME LEARNING. THERE WAS EVEN "GRUMBLING IN THE RANKS" ABOUT THE COMPUTER BEING "LOSER-FRIENDLY."

THEN ONE DAY THE SCIENTIST WHO HAD INVENTED THE COMPUTER, WHO WAS NAMED EUGENE (WHAT ELSE?), CAME TO GET "SOME USER FEEDBACK."

HIS FIRST QUESTION WAS:

A: IS THIS COMPUTER "USER-FRIENDLY"?
OR
B: WOULD YOU RATHER BE AN ARTILLERY TARGET?

HERE ARE SOME ACTUAL ANSWERS THE SOLDIERS GAVE:

"OH YES, OL 17,000 EYES IS VERY USER-FRIENDLY. ONLY PROBLEMS ARE STUPID HUMAN ONES. LIKE TOUCHING HOT BULBS AND WHAT NOT."

"BULBS BURN OUT, BUT NOT COMPUTER'S FAULT. BELIEVE IT'S CAUSED BY MOTHS—ATTRACTED TO THE LIGHT, YOU KNOW. THEY FLY IN AND ZAP! CAUSE ALL THE PROBLEMS!"

"AGREE WITH HIM, THE COMPUTER IS FINE—IT JUST HAS A FEW 'BUGS'! AND I AM EUGENE-FRIENDLY. HI, EUGENE!"

FROM THESE ANSWERS YOU SEE THAT TWO IMPORTANT CONCEPTS HAVE BEEN, YOU MIGHT SAY, "INVENTED":

ONE: THE COMPUTER IS "USER-FRIENDLY."

TWO: COMPUTER ERRORS ARE CAUSED BY "BUGS."

MEANWHILE, EUGENE WAS TURNING IN HIS REPORT, IN WHICH HE CONCLUDED—

"USERS MAKING STUPID ERRORS, APPEAR UNRELIABLE, ALLOWED BUGS TO ENTER COMPUTER ROOM. POSSIBLE DANGER TO COMPUTER. SUGGEST FINDING BETTER USERS. SEND THESE USERS TO OPERATE SOMETHING SAFE, LIKE ARTILLERY."

AND NOW THE STAGE HAD BEEN SET FOR ...

A BRIEF HISTORY OF GEEK TIME

NEAR-SIGHTED, INFORMALLY DRESSED, WITH UNCONVENTIONAL SOCIAL INSTINCTS, EARLY GEEKS, AS YOU MIGHT IMAGINE, WERE NOT READILY ACCEPTED INTO THE WORKPLACE ... PRIOR TO THE INVENTION OF THE COMPUTER.

THERE'S PROBABLY A VERY RATIONAL EXPLANATION FOR THIS

AS A RESULT, THEY OFTEN HAD TO TAKE WHATEVER WORK WAS AVAILABLE, SUCH AS BITING THE HEADS OFF OF LIVE CHICKENS IN CARNIVAL SIDESHOWS.

WHILE THE WORK WAS UNDERPAID, IT WAS AT LEAST LESS REPETITIVE THAN THE COMPUTER ANALYSIS THEY WOULD LATER DO, AND THERE WAS PLENTY TO EAT.

ALSO, BEING A CARNIVAL PERFORMER BROUGHT A CERTAIN DISTINCTION TO THE GEEK NAME.

EVEN TODAY SOME OLD-TIMERS WILL GREET A GEEK BY SAYING, "YOU'RE A GEEK? WAS THAT YOU I SAW OVER IN THE COUNTY FAIR IN '48?"

THE GEEK AND UNCLE SAM

HOWEVER, WITH THE INVENTION OF THE USER-FRIENDLY COMPUTER, AND EVEN MORE IMPORTANTLY, OF THE COMPUTER BUG, A COUPLE OF THINGS HAPPENED.

FIRST, SOME OF THE GEEKS WORKING IN THE CARNIVAL HEARD ABOUT THE ARMY'S PROBLEM WITH BUGS, AND THEY THOUGHT— IF THEY COULD EAT CHICKENS, THEY SHOULD BE ABLE TO SWALLOW A FEW COMPUTER "BUGS."

SO THEY ENLISTED, AND IN A SHORT TIME PROVED TO BE SO GOOD AT RIDDING THE ARMY OF ITS COMPUTER BUGS THAT THE ARMY BEGAN RECRUITING MORE GEEKS, WITH POSTERS THAT WOULD LATER BECOME FAMOUS. AND SOON GEEKS EVERYWHERE WERE PUTTING DOWN THEIR CHICKENS AND HEADING OFF TO KEEP THE WORLD SAFE FOR DEMOCRACY.

THE ARMY WANTS YOU, GEEK!

GEEK HISTORIANS NOW BELIEVE THERE IS A DIRECT LINE BETWEEN THESE EARLY GEEKS AND THE "CGI JOE" (SEE PAGE 161) STILL IN EXISTENCE TODAY.

DO YOU . . . SAY THE COMPUTER IS "USER-FRIENDLY"?

GEEKSPEAK

GEEKSPEAK: THE TRICKY DOUBLE MEANINGS OF GEEKS– GEEK DOUBLESPEAK.

IT'S A LOT LIKE HAVING A FRIEND

A FRIEND WITH SOME SERIOUS EMOTIONAL PROBLEMS

THAT ONLY MAKE THE FRIENDSHIP STRONGER.

IN NEWBIE TERMS

IT REMINDS ME OF BEING EATEN BY A SHARK.

HONEY, YOU WERE NEVER EATEN BY A SHARK.

OH NO? WHAT ABOUT PETERSON, MY NEW BOSS?

THERE IS THE SAME LOOK OF DOOM IN YOUR EYES,

AND THE WAY I CRY OUT, "OH NO I'M GOING DOWN."

AND NO ONE WILL HELP.

THE 7 HABITS OF HIGHLY EFFECTIVE COMPUTER GEEKS

DO YOU ...
SWEAR
"LIKE A PIRATE"?

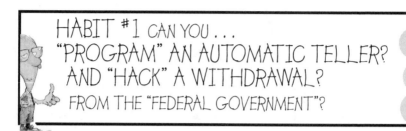

HABIT #1 CAN YOU . . .
"PROGRAM" AN AUTOMATIC TELLER? +2
AND "HACK" A WITHDRAWAL? +4
FROM THE "FEDERAL GOVERNMENT"? +2

ANYONE WHO CAN PUNCH THE CORRECT KEYS AT AN AUTOMATIC TELLER—AND THIS INCLUDES THOSE WHO FAIL IN MANY FIRST ATTEMPTS—IS "PROGRAMMING" A COMPUTER. BECAUSE AN AUTOMATIC TELLER IS ACTUALLY A COMPUTER, JUST PRETENDING TO BE A KIND OF STINGY STEPPARENT.

YOU MAY HAVE FOUND THAT, IF YOU SPEND ENOUGH TIME AT THE AUTOMATIC TELLER, YOU CAN EVEN PROGRAM A WITHDRAWAL WHEN YOU HAVE NO MONEY—SIMPLY BY PUSHING KEYS BY ACCIDENT. PROGRAMMING LIKE THIS, BY PUSHING KEYS BY ACCIDENT, IS CALLED "HACKING." THE FACT THAT HACKING IS ILLEGAL MEANS, TECHNICALLY, YOU COULD GO TO JAIL, BY ACCIDENT. OF COURSE, THIS NEVER SEEMS TO STOP YOU WHEN YOU REALLY NEED A CHEESEBURGER.

AND IF YOU'RE THE PERSON WHO IS ALWAYS SPENDING WAY TOO MUCH TIME AT THE AUTOMATIC TELLER, TYING UP THE WHOLE LINE, THEN YOU'RE PROBABLY "HACKING" INTO THE "FEDERAL GOVERNMENT" BANK ACCOUNT—TRYING TO MAKE A WITHDRAWAL, EVEN THOUGH THE GOVERNMENT HAS NO MONEY.

HABIT #2 DO YOU ...
LOSE TRACK OF "TIME"?
AND THE DIFFERENCE BETWEEN "MONDAY
AND THURSDAY"?
BUT NEVER "STAR YEARS"?

+2
+2
+4

WHEN YOU'RE PROGRAMMING, OR HACKING, OR STANDING IN FRONT OF AN AUTOMATIC TELLER, PUSHING KEYS BY ACCIDENT, IT IS QUITE EASY TO LOSE TRACK OF "TIME." IN FACT, EINSTEIN COULD HAVE COME UP WITH HIS THEORY, "TIME IS RELATIVE," A LOT MORE EASILY, IF HE JUST HAD A COMPUTER TO HACK ON.

AND ONCE THE THEORY THAT "TIME IS RELATIVE" HAS BEEN PROVEN TO YOUR SATISFACTION, BY LOSING TRACK OF A FEW HOURS WHILE ON THE COMPUTER, EVEN THE DIFFERENCE BETWEEN "MONDAY AND THURSDAY" SUDDENLY STARTS TO SEEM A LOT LESS CLEAR.

OF COURSE, THE GREAT THING ABOUT "STAR YEARS" IS—

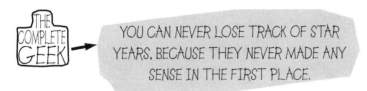

THE COMPLETE GEEK → YOU CAN NEVER LOSE TRACK OF STAR YEARS, BECAUSE THEY NEVER MADE ANY SENSE IN THE FIRST PLACE.

63

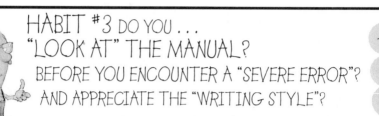

HABIT #3 DO YOU ...
"LOOK AT" THE MANUAL?
BEFORE YOU ENCOUNTER A "SEVERE ERROR"?
AND APPRECIATE THE "WRITING STYLE"?

+2
·
+3
·
+4

"LOOKING AT" THE MANUAL ALWAYS TELLS THE GEEK A LOT OF THINGS ABOUT THE COMPUTER. FOR EXAMPLE, AN ENORMOUS MANUAL MEANS THE COMPUTER IS GENEROUS AND USER-FRIENDLY. A MANUAL THAT IS MEAN AND THIN MEANS THE COMPUTER REALLY MEANS BUSINESS. AND A MANUAL THAT IS IN A FOREIGN LANGUAGE MEANS THE GEEK HAS SOMEHOW TRAVELED TO A FOREIGN COUNTRY.

ALSO, THE GEEK ALWAYS MAKES SURE TO LOOK AT THE MANUAL BEFORE DOING THE COMPUTER REAL DAMAGE. BECAUSE AFTERWARD THE MANUAL IS JUST TOO FRIGHTENING—THE WAY IT ALWAYS SAYS NOT TO DO THE THING THAT WAS JUST DONE, AS IF IT KNEW, AND THEN CALLS THIS A "SEVERE ERROR," WHICH MEANS THAT RATHER THAN MORE RAM BEING PUT IN, THERE WAS A SLIPUP AND AN APPENDIX WAS TAKEN OUT.

FINALLY, IF YOU APPRECIATE THE "WRITING STYLE" OF A MANUAL, YOU ARE OBVIOUSLY A GEEK WORKING AS A "TECHNICAL WRITER"—AND YOU BELIEVE THAT "LENGTHY CONCATENATIONS OF IMPOSSIBLY COMPLEX JARGON (SUCH AS THIS ONE)" CAN HAVE "WRITING STYLE," IF DONE CORRECTLY.

HABIT #4 DO YOU ...
CALL COMPUTER ERRORS "FEATURES"?
AND IF NOT, THEY'RE "HUMAN ERROR"?
AND IF NOT, THEY'RE "HUMAN ERROR"?

+4
+2
+4

IF YOU CALL COMPUTER ERRORS "FEATURES," YOU ARE A GEEK WORKING IN "MARKETING," YOUR JOB IS TO SELL PRODUCTS THAT ARE BOTH FLAWED AND POORLY UNDERSTOOD. AND THIS YOU TURN TO YOUR ADVANTAGE BY SAYING, OF ANY FLAW, "WE <u>MEANT</u> TO DO THAT."

IF YOU BELIEVE ALL COMPUTER ERRORS ARE CAUSED BY "HUMAN ERROR" YOU MUST BE A GEEK WORKING IN "TECHNICAL SUPPORT." YOUR JOB IS TO LISTEN ALL DAY TO ERRORS SO STUPID THAT ONLY TRULY CREATIVE HUMANS COULD BE THE CAUSE—SUCH AS THE PERSON WHO TOOK THE BACK OFF THE MONITOR TO GET THE BUGS OUT, OR THE PERSON WHO USED THE MOUSE AS A FOOTPEDAL.

OF COURSE, HUMANS NOT ONLY CAUSE ALL ERRORS, THEY ALSO IMMEDIATELY FORGET THAT THEY DID, AND BURY THE ERRORS DEEP IN THE SUBCONSCIOUS, SO THAT A GOD-LIKE OMNISCIENCE IS THEN NEEDED TO FIND OUT WHAT THE HELL HAPPENED.

THE COMPLETE GEEK ➔ TO ERR IS HUMAN, TO FIND THE ERROR, DIVINE.

65

HABIT #5 DO YOU . . .   +2
FEEL SUPPORTED BY "TECHNICAL SUPPORT"?
FEEL HELD WHEN YOU'RE "ON HOLD"?   +3
CALL 911 AND ASK FOR SOMEONE "TECHNICAL"?   +4

WHEN YOU CALL "TECHNICAL SUPPORT" IS IT LIKE OLD
GEEK WEEK? DO YOU STRIKE UP A CONVERSATION ABOUT WHO HAD
COLD PIZZA LAST NIGHT, AND WHO WORKED LATER THAN WHO.
AND WHO HAD COLD PIZZA FOR BREAKFAST, AND SO ON? UNTIL YOU
FORGET WHAT YOU WERE CALLING FOR, AND HANG UP. AND THEN
YOU HAVE TO CALL BACK, AND WAIT 2 HOURS ON HOLD. BUT THAT'S
OK BECAUSE . . .

HAVE SOME OF YOUR BEST MEMORIES OCCURRED WHILE YOU
WAITED 2 HOURS "ON HOLD"—HOPING TO FIND THAT ONE TRUE
GEEK SOULMATE WHO MIGHT HAVE AN ANSWER FOR YOUR TRIVIAL
TECHNICAL QUESTION? CAN YOU EVEN REMEMBER THE SONG THAT
WAS PLAYING WHILE YOU WERE ON HOLD? AND HOW MANY TIMES
IT PLAYED OVER . . . AND COME TO THINK OF IT, EVEN HOW
FRUSTRATED YOU WERE? AND . . . AFTER THAT YOUR MEMORY STARTS
TO GET BLURRY?

AND WHEN YOU CALL 911, ARE YOU INTERESTED IN TALKING, NOT TO
WHOEVER HAPPENS TO ANSWER THE PHONE, BUT TO SOMEONE
"TECHNICAL"? A QUALIFIED NEUROSURGEON, AT LEAST?

HABIT #6 DO YOU ...
DO THAT "COMPUTER THING"? +2
WITHOUT EXPENDING "NOTICEABLE" EFFORT? +2
WITHOUT "KNOWING" EXACTLY WHAT YOU DID? +4

BASICALLY, CAN YOU SOLVE ALMOST ANY COMMON COMPUTER PROBLEM, IN A VAGUE SORT OF OFFHANDED WAY—SUCH AS ENTERING THE ROOM—WHILE TRYING YOUR BEST NOT TO MAKE THE PERSON HAVING THE PROBLEM FEEL LIKE AN IDIOT—BECAUSE:

GEEKS DON'T RUB IT IN.

OTHER WAYS OF DOING "THAT COMPUTER THING," ALONG WITH MERELY "ENTERING THE ROOM," INCLUDE—ASKING THAT THE PROBLEM BE REPEATED, TYPING A FEW SEEMINGLY RANDOM COMMANDS, OR SIMPLY PRONOUNCING THE PROBLEM "SOLVED." ALL OF THESE WAYS ARE VALID, SINCE AT NO TIME IS THE GEEK REQUIRED TO EXPEND "NOTICEABLE" EFFORT.

THE HIGHEST FORM OF DOING THE "COMPUTER THING" INVOLVES A PURELY ZEN-LIKE STATE, IN WHICH THE GEEK DOES NOT "KNOW," EXACTLY, WHAT WAS DONE TO SOLVE THE PROBLEM. BUT ONLY TRUE ALPHA GEEKS, WHO HOLD THE HIGHEST RANK IN GEEKDOM, EVER POSSESS THIS RARE ABILITY.

HABIT #7 DO YOU ...
SWEAR "LIKE A PIRATE"?
WHEN YOU ARE AT "WIT'S END"?
AND THEN APOLOGIZE "PROFUSELY"?

+2

+2

+4

GEEKS SWEAR "LIKE PIRATES." THE REASON IS THAT BOTH
GEEKS AND PIRATES ARE REQUIRED TO PERFORM HIGHLY
ADVANCED TECHNICAL FEATS. SUCH AS PIRATING SOFTWARE
AND LOWERING THE BOOM. AND, OF COURSE—

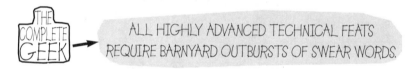

ALL HIGHLY ADVANCED TECHNICAL FEATS
REQUIRE BARNYARD OUTBURSTS OF SWEAR WORDS.

IN FACT, THE ONLY REAL DIFFERENCE BETWEEN GEEKS AND
PIRATES IS THAT PIRATES SWEAR JUST BECAUSE THEY'RE
PIRATES—WHILE GEEKS ONLY SWEAR WHEN THEY HAVE
REACHED "WIT'S END." PIRATES DO ARGUE, THOUGH, THAT
GEEKS HAVE NO "WIT" TO BEGIN WITH, AS FAR AS THE PIRATES
CAN TELL.

ONE OTHER MINOR DISTINCTION BETWEEN GEEKS AND PIRATES
IS THAT GEEKS APOLOGIZE "PROFUSELY" WHEN THEY HAVE
FINISHED SWEARING, WHILE PIRATES MERELY APOLOGIZE.

THE IDENTIFICATION OF GEEKS WITH PIRATES IS SO STRONG THAT
ONE GROUP OF GEEKS—WHO BECAME FAMOUS FOR DEVELOPING
THE "GRAPHICAL INTERFACE" FOR APPLE COMPUTERS—EVEN
CALLED THEMSELVES "PIRATES," AND FLEW A PIRATE FLAG OVER
THE BUILDING WHERE THEY WERE WORKING. HOWEVER, THE
BUILDING DID NOT SET SAIL QUITE AS THEY EXPECTED, NO MATTER
HOW MUCH SWEARING THEY DID.

THE COMPUTER GEEK'S PRECISE USE OF SWEAR WORDS, OR
EXPLETIVES, AS PIRATES CALL THEM, TYPICALLY GOES LIKE THIS:

"THIS GOSHDARNED PIECE OF
CRAP REALLY BLOWS. IF THIS
DOESN'T WORK I'M TOTALLY
SCREWED. OH PHOOEY.
OH MOTHER PHOOEY.
OOOH—AND NOW IT
WORKS! ... TITS!"

THE 7 EXPLETIVES OF
HIGHLY EFFECTIVE
COMPUTER GEEKS

GOSHDARNED
PIECE OF CRAP
REALLY BLOWS
TOTALLY SCREWED
OH PHOOEY
MOTHER-PHOOEY
(AND)
OOOH—TITS! (ONLY USED IN
A GOOD WAY)

ELECTRONIC JOURNAL OF BILL G/

12/31/99 8:45 AM PST

STILL WAITING FOR ZEKE'S RETURN. DECIDE
TO WORK. NEW MILLENNIUM EVE, BUT NOTHING
ELSE TO DO. DONE THIS BEFORE — WORK
WHILE OTHERS TAKE HOLIDAY OR SLEEP. THIS
IS EDGE. STEAL INTO HOMES OF COMPETITORS,
WHEN UNSUSPECTING. TAKE AWAY PRECIOUS
ADVANTAGES GOTTEN DURING "BUSINESS
HOURS." WORK LIKE ANY TEN GEEKS. WORK
LIKE NO GEEK HAS EVER WORKED BEFORE. NO
GEEK EXCEPT MAYBE ZEKE.

ZEKE IS ROAMING INTERNET AT SUPER SPEEDS.
TRACKING MOVEMENTS: SILICON VALLEY, LOS
ANGELES, CHICAGO, NEW YORK, LONDON, BONN,
BOMBAY, TOKYO, BOURNE.

BUT WHEN ZEKE STOPS, MAKE A NOTE: BILL
WILL BE WAITING.

THE "GQ" BASIC QUESTION
#7
ARE YOU...
OBSESSIVE/COMPULSIVE
ABOUT "WORK"?

THE MIGRANT APPLE PICKER   75

71

GQ #7.1 ARE YOU . . .
OBSESSIVE/COMPULSIVE
ABOUT "WORK"?

+4

OF COURSE, THIS IS NOT MEANT IN A BAD WAY.
TRUE, IN OTHER PURSUITS, SUCH AS PATIENT IN A MENTAL WARD,
BEING OBSESSIVE/COMPULSIVE MIGHT BE TREATED
DIFFERENTLY, EVEN WITH MEDICATION.

BUT WHEN IT COMES TO YOUR "WORK," YOUR ABILITY TO
OBSESS ON DETAILS AS BIG-PICTURE, AND AS FUN TO WORK
WITH, AS THE ANATOMICAL PARTS OF A GNAT, IS THE REAL
SECRET BEHIND ALL YOUR MOST COMPULSIVE
ACCOMPLISHMENTS.

BESIDES, THOSE ANATOMICAL PARTS DON'T SEEM SO
COMPULSIVE TO GNATS, OR TO PEOPLE WITH BRAINS THE SAME
SIZE AS GNATS, WHO HAPPEN TO BE HEADING UP YOUR COMPANY.
AND THEY'RE THE ONES YOU'RE HOPING TO IMPRESS. THE
GNATS ARE. THERE'S NO IMPRESSING PEOPLE WITH BRAINS
THAT SMALL.

GQ #7.2 DO YOU ...
CONFUSE WORK WITH "PLAY"?
STILL HOPING TO "PLEASE" YOUR PARENTS?
OR ELSE A QUALIFIED "PROFESSIONAL"?

+2
+2
+3

WHEN SOMEONE ASKS, "SO, WHAT DID YOU DO TODAY?" ARE YOU LIKELY TO ANSWER, "WELL, I 'PLAYED' AROUND WITH [JARGON FOLLOWS FOR BORING TASK]"? DO YOU FREELY ADMIT, "METHINKS I DOTH LIKE WORK TOO MUCH"?

THE TENDENCY FOR A GEEK TO CONFUSE WORK WITH "PLAY" USUALLY STARTS WHEN THE GEEK FIRST BEGINS WORKING, SOMETIME IN INFANCY. THE GEEK'S PARENTS WHO NOTICE THEIR CHILD HAS A STRANGE LOOK OF OBSESSIVE-COMPULSIVENESS, PRETEND TO BE "PLEASED," SAYING, "OH LOOK, OUR BABY IS PLAYING."

THIS CONFUSION OF WORK WITH PLAY CONTINUES UNTIL LATER IN LIFE, WHEN THE GEEK BEGINS TO "PLAY" WITH QUALIFIED "PROFESSIONALS," SUCH AS CO-WORKERS, THERAPISTS, AND HAIR-STYLISTS, WHOSE JOB IT IS TO PRETEND TO BE "PLEASED."

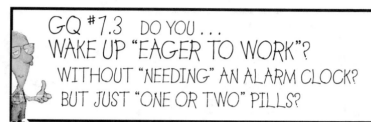

GQ #7.3 DO YOU . . .
WAKE UP "EAGER TO WORK"?   +3
WITHOUT "NEEDING" AN ALARM CLOCK?   +2
BUT JUST "ONE OR TWO" PILLS?   +2

WAKING UP "EAGER TO WORK" IS A PRETTY CLEAR INDICATOR OF HIGHER GEEKINESS—OR ELSE, OF HOLDING DOWN THE JOB OF ROYALTY IN A SMALL PRINCIPALITY BY THE SEA.

A LITTLE KNOWN FACT ABOUT GEEKS IS THAT THEY CAN WAKE UP FOR WORK EVEN WITHOUT "NEEDING" AN ALARM CLOCK. THERE ARE TWO SCIENTIFIC EXPLANATIONS FOR THIS: 1) THEY GO TO WORK LATE, 2) THEY HAVE SOMEONE TO WAKE THEM UP, WHO HAS AN ALARM CLOCK.

ALL THAT GEEKS REALLY NEED ARE JUST "ONE OR TWO"—OR AT THE MOST, A HANDFUL, OR TWO—OF PRESCRIPTIONS, VITAMINS, RELAXERS, STIMULANTS, AND POSSIBLY DRUG-TRIAL PLACEBOS, TO REALLY START THE DAY OFF RIGHT.

THE MIGRANT APPLE PICKER

ONCE I WENT FOR A JOB, AS A "MIGRANT APPLE PICKER."

I FIGURED I WOULD BE GREAT AT IT. APPLES ARE MY FAVORITE. THEY'RE WAY BETTER THAN OTHER COMPUTERS.

PLUS, I LIKE AN HONEST JOB TITLE. I MEAN, "MIGRANT APPLE PICKER" REALLY SAYS IT ALL. ANY OTHER TITLE THAT YOU MIGHT EXPECT, LIKE "TEMPORARY QUALITY CONTROL," WOULD BE JUST A LOT OF CORPORATE-SPEAK.

MY ONLY PROBLEM WAS, IT WAS DAMN HARD TO FIND THE FACILITY. ALL YOU COULD SEE WAS A LOT OF TREES.

NOW I KNEW THE COMPANY HAD FALLEN ON HARD TIMES. BUT THIS—IT KIND OF MADE YOU FEEL WALL STREET'S PAIN.

FINALLY I FOUND A GUY AT THE FRONT GATE. SINCE HE WAS JUST STANDING AROUND I FIGURED HE HAD TO BE A SECURITY GUARD, OR MANAGEMENT.

I WENT UP TO HIM AND SAID, "I'M HERE FOR THE APPLE-PICKER POSITION."

HE LOOKED AT ME FOR A SECOND, AND THEN HE SAID, "WHAT ARE YOU, SOME SORT OF GEEK?"

RIGHT THEN I KNEW—THREATENED BY INDIVIDUALITY. MUST BE MANAGEMENT. SO I STARTED TALKING TO HIM, LIKE I ALWAYS

TALK TO MANAGEMENT, REAL CLEAR AND LOUD. "WELL, WHERE WILL I BE WORKING?" I SAID, THE WAY YOU MIGHT TALK NORMALLY TO AN IDIOT.

HE ANSWERED ME IN THE SAME TONE. "IN A TREE," HE SAID. THAT'S THE WAY MANAGEMENT TALKS, TOO. IN FACT HAVING A CONVERSATION WITH MANAGEMENT IS PRETTY MUCH A BATTLE OF IDIOTS THE WHOLE WAY.

AT FIRST, I DIDN'T EVEN KNOW WHAT HE MEANT. THEN IT HIT ME. A TREE—THAT WAS ANOTHER NAME FOR THE PECKING ORDER, MANAGEMENT AT THE TOP, EVERYBODY ELSE AT THE BOTTOM.

TO LET HIM KNOW I GOT HIS DRIFT, I SAID, "EXACTLY ... AND WHERE IN THE TREE?"

AND THEN HE GOT A REAL SERIOUS LOOK, LIKE I HAD ASKED A TOUGH MANAGEMENT QUESTION. "WELL," HE SAID, "MOST WORKERS START AT THE TOP AND WORK THEIR WAY TO THE BOTTOM."

I THOUGHT TO MYSELF, THAT'S REFRESHING. MANAGEMENT THAT TELLS THE TRUTH. BUT THE TRUTH WAS, I WAS STARTING TO GET ANNOYED.

"SO TRUE, SO TRUE," I SAID TO HIM, STILL REAL CLEAR AND LOUD, "BUT, WHICH TREE, EXACTLY?"

"WELL, YOU <u>PICK IT</u>," HE SAID. WITH THAT, HE STARTED LAUGHING LIKE HELL.

I WAS ABOUT TO START LAUGHING, TOO, BECAUSE THAT'S WHAT YOU HAVE TO DO, WHEN YOU TALK TO MANAGEMENT. YOU HAVE TO LAUGH WHEN THEY DO, EVEN WHEN THERE'S NOT A DAMN THING FUNNY ABOUT IT..

BUT THEN I THOUGHT, SCREW IT. I'M NOT LAUGHING ANYMORE.

"NO, I'M NOT GOING TO <u>PICK IT</u>," I SAID BACK TO HIM. AND THEN I USED THE FOUR LETTER WORD I HAD NEVER HAD THE NERVE TO USE BEFORE. "I QUIT," I SAID.

AS SOON AS I SAID THAT, HE GOT A KNOT IN HIS BROW. IT REMINDED ME EXACTLY OF THAT STORY, "A&P," BY JOHN UPDIKE, WHEN THE STORE MANAGER GETS A KNOT IN HIS BROW, RIGHT WHEN THE KID QUITS.

LET ME TELL YOU, HE WAS PRETTY SURPRISED. ALL HE COULD DO WAS LOOK AT ME REAL STRANGE, AS IF HE HADN'T HEARD ME OR SOMETHING.

TO BE HONEST, I WAS KIND OF SURPRISED MYSELF. GEEZ, I HADN'T EVEN GIVEN HIM MY RESUMÉ YET. I STILL HAD IT IN MY HAND, AND IT WAS FEELING A LITTLE WARM—AND NOT BECAUSE IT JUST CAME OFF THE COPIER, EITHER.

SO I TOLD HIM AGAIN, "I SAID, I QUIT." I THOUGHT SAYING IT AGAIN MIGHT CALM ME DOWN. I GET NERVOUS AS HELL IN CERTAIN SITUATIONS. AND LATER, WHEN I THOUGHT ABOUT ALL THIS, I WAS GLAD I DID SAY IT AGAIN. I MEAN, YOU DON'T GET THAT MANY CHANCES IN LIFE TO SAY THAT SORT OF THING.

BUT NOW HE LOOKED AT ME LIKE HE WAS THE ONE GETTING WARM. AND I COULD TELL HE WAS GOING TO SAY SOMETHING SMART—WHICH, WITH HIM BEING A MANAGEMENT TYPE, WASN'T ALL THAT EASY. I HAD TO GIVE HIM A SECOND, AND THEN HE FINALLY SAID, "WHAT ARE YOU, SOME SORT OF PSYCHO?"

"YEAH, THAT'S RIGHT," I SAID. AND HONESTLY, I COULD ALMOST SEE HIS POINT. "I'M A REAL PSYCHO-GEEK."

THEN I TURNED AROUND AND STARTED TO BEAT IT, RIGHT THE HELL OUT OF THERE. OVER MY SHOULDER, THOUGH, JUST FOR THE EFFECT, I SAID, "BUT IT'S TOO BAD. THIS COMPANY REALLY NEEDS PEOPLE LIKE ME, THAT ARE PSYCHO-GEEKS." I WAS TRYING TO BE DRAMATIC AND ALL, SO I WOULD REMEMBER THE MOMENT.

AND THE VERY LAST THING I SAID WAS—ACTUALLY, I SORT OF SHOUTED IT, ON THE SLIGHT CHANCE THAT EVEN OLD STEVE JOBS COULD HEAR ME, THROUGH ALL THOSE DAMN TREES— "APPLES FOREVER."

ARE YOU ... OBSESSIVE/COMPULSIVE ABOUT "WORK"?

GEEKSPEAK

GEEKSPEAK: THE TRICKY DOUBLE MEANINGS OF GEEKS– GEEK DOUBLESPEAK.

TO BE IS TO DO — PLATO

TO DO IS TO BE — ARISTOTLE

IN NEWBIE TERMS

DO-BE-DO-BE-DO I LOVE DOING EXPENSE REPORTS

SINATRA, I THINK

THE "GQ" BASIC QUESTION
6

DO YOU...
HAVE A HIGH REGARD FOR "THE BRAIN"?

WILLIAM G

GQ #6.1 DO YOU ...
HAVE A HIGH REGARD FOR "THE
BRAIN"?

+4

WHAT IS "THE BRAIN" TO YOU? IS IT AN ORGAN FOR PROCESSING AND DIGESTING NOT SO DIFFERENT FROM THE LIVER OR EVEN THE YOU-KNOW-WHAT? OR IS IT A SYMBOL FOR THE UNKNOWN, THE STILL UNSEEN, THE FOREVER UNDYING HOPE THAT YOU MIGHT STILL BE PROVEN RIGHT IN ALL THE ARGUMENTS YOU'VE EVER LOST?

TO A GEEK

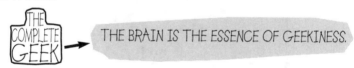

THE BRAIN IS THE ESSENCE OF GEEKINESS.

THE BRAIN IS THE VERY THING THAT MAKES YOU WHO YOU ARE—YOUR UNIQUE SIGNATURE, YOUR MENTAL THUMBPRINT AND YOUR DISTINCTIVE ERROR-PRONENESS ALL ROLLED UP INTO ONE GRAY MASS WITH MORE WRINKLES THAN A TYPICAL ROLE-PLAYING FANTASY ON THE INTERNET.

WHICH LEADS TO THE QUESTION ...

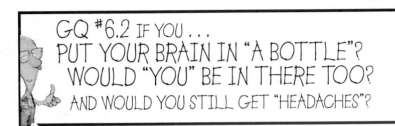

GQ #6.2 IF YOU ...
PUT YOUR BRAIN IN "A BOTTLE"?
WOULD "YOU" BE IN THERE TOO?
AND WOULD YOU STILL GET "HEADACHES"?

+2

+3

+4

THE BRAIN IN "A BOTTLE" IS ONE OF THE GREATEST PARADOXES IN GEEK LORE—IS IT POSSIBLE THAT YOUR BRAIN COULD BE PUT IN A BOTTLE, AND CONTINUE TO BE "YOU." OR WOULD THE BOTTLE START TO HAVE SECOND THOUGHTS AND SELF-DOUBT, SUCH AS "AM I SACRIFICING TOO MUCH FOR THE CAUSE OF SCIENCE?"

THIS QUESTION HAS NEVER BEEN RESOLVED, THOUGH NOT FOR LACK OF BOTTLES. THE PROBLEM HAS BEEN THAT SCIENTISTS HAVE NOT BEEN ABLE TO FIGURE OUT HOW TO GET THE BRAIN INSIDE OF SOMETHING THE SIZE OF A BOTTLENECK. IT TURNS OUT TO BE A LOT TRICKIER THAN GETTING A MODEL SHIP IN THERE.

"HEADACHES" SUCH AS THIS COULD PROBABLY BE AVOIDED IF THE BRAIN WAS NO LONGER INSIDE THE HEAD. BUT EVEN INSIDE A BOTTLE THE BRAIN WOULD STILL FACE SERIOUS DISCOMFORTS, SUCH AS FEELING SHATTERED AND GOING TO PIECES.

GQ #6.3 DO YOU ...
BELIEVE THE BRAIN IS A "MUSCLE"? +2
THAT JUST NEEDS "BRAIN FOOD"? +3
AND A "GOOD NIGHT'S SLEEP" WHEN YOU THINK TOO HARD? +4

THE BELIEF THAT THE BRAIN IS A "MUSCLE" BEGINS IN A GEEK'S
CHILDHOOD, PERHAPS BECAUSE THE GEEK IS LESS MUSCULAR
THAN OTHER CHILDREN. THERE IS A GRAY WRINKLY MUSCLE, THE
GEEK BEGINS TO BELIEVE, JUST ABOVE THE EYEBROWS—GROWING
QUITE NICELY, THANK YOU VERY MUCH—BUT JUST NOT ON THE
OUTSIDE LIKE OTHER MUSCLES, ON OTHER CHILDREN.

SOON THE GEEK ALSO LEARNS THAT DOING THINGS LIKE
READING BOOKS, STUDYING AT SCHOOL, AND SETTING UP
COMPUTERS, SEEMS TO HELP THE BRAIN TO GROW—BECAUSE
ADULTS DON'T DO THESE THINGS, AND THEIR BRAINS HAVE
STOPPED GROWING. THESE THINGS THE GEEK CHILD CALLS
"BRAIN FOOD."

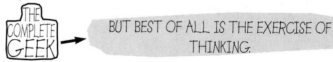

BUT BEST OF ALL IS THE EXERCISE OF
THINKING.

THE GEEK LEARNS, TOO, THAT THE BRAIN ALSO NEEDS MANY
HOURS SPENT DWELLING IN THE IMAGINATION, AND THINKING SO
HARD THAT, AFTERWARD, IN A PEACEFUL EXHAUSTION, THE GEEK
CHILD FALLS OFF TO A "GOOD NIGHT'S SLEEP"—ALL OF
WHICH ARE MORE THINGS ADULTS NEVER SEEM TO DO.

GQ #6.4 DO YOU BELIEVE...
WITH BRAINS, LESS IS NOT "MORE"?
AND "BIG" IS NOT BETTER?
IT'S REALLY "WRINKLES" THAT COUNT?

+2

+2

+4

FOR THE GEEK, ALMOST ANY PROBLEM CAN BE SOLVED BY ONE SIMPLE SOLUTION: IF THE GEEK ONLY HAD "MORE" BRAINS.

WHAT HAPPENS, THOUGH, WHEN THE PROBLEM IS, TOO MUCH BRAINS? DOES THE BRAIN JUST BURST THROUGH THE SKULL AT THE EARS? AND WHAT ABOUT CREATURES WITH REALLY "BIG" BRAINS, SUCH AS ELEPHANTS, DINOSAURS AND 7 FOOT BASKETBALL CENTERS—WHY ARE THEY NOT TERRIBLY GOOD AT SOLVING PROBLEMS?

THE GEEK'S ANSWER IS—ELEPHANTS, DINOSAURS AND 7 FOOT CENTERS HAVE REALLY SMOOTH BRAINS. AND IT'S REALLY "WRINKLES" THAT COUNT. WRINKLES, AS PREVIOUSLY MENTIONED, ARE THE TWISTS AND TURNS IN THE TYPICAL PLOT OF AN INTERNET ROLE-PLAYING FANTASY—THEY ARE ALSO A WAY THE BRAIN CAN REMEMBER ALL THOSE TWISTS AND TURNS, WITHOUT ACTUALLY OUTGROWING THE CRANIUM, JUST WHEN THE DINOSAUR IS ABOUT TO CRUSH THE 7 FOOT 6 MIDGET.

85

GQ #6.5 DO YOU . . .
HAVE MORE BOOKS THAN "LOOKS"? +2
MORE BOOKS THAN "MONEY"? +3
MORE BOOKS THAN FIT IN A "MOVING VAN"? +4

GEEKS HAVE MORE BOOKS THAN "LOOKS." THIS IS A
STRAIGHTFORWARD NOTION THAT DOESN'T NEED A LOT OF
EXPLAINING—UNLESS YOU HAPPEN TO HAVE MORE LOOKS
THAN BOOKS, AND THEN IT PROBABLY <u>DOES</u> NEED A LOT OF
EXPLAINING, MORE THAN CAN FIT HERE, IN JUST ONE BOOK.

THE SAYING—

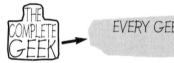

EVERY GEEK IS RICH WHO ONLY HAS
BOOKS.

—HAS HELD TRUE, IN DIFFERENT VARIATIONS, FOR THOUSANDS
OF YEARS. IT EVEN HOLDS TRUE NO MATTER HOW MUCH
"MONEY" YOU ACTUALLY HAVE—AND DEPENDS ONLY ON
HOW MUCH VALUE YOU PLACE ON YOUR BOOKS.

WHEREVER THEY LIVE, GEEKS WOULD REALLY PREFER, IF AT
ALL POSSIBLE, TO STAY—SIMPLY TO AVOID HAVING TO MOVE
ALL THEIR BOOKS. THE "MOVING VAN" HAS NOT YET
BEEN MADE THAT CAN HOLD ALL OF A GEEK'S BOOKS. THE
VANS KEEP GETTING BIGGER, AND GEEKS KEEP GETTING
MORE BOOKS.

GQ #6.6 DO YOU ...
"LEARN SOMETHING NEW" EVERY DAY? +2
AND "PAY FOR IT" WITH LARGE SUMS OF MONEY? +3
BUT STILL REMEMBER YOUR "ALMA MATER" FONDLY? +2

"LEARNING SOMETHING NEW" ALWAYS BRINGS THE GEEK THE MOST PRIZED OF POSSESSIONS, A THING THAT IS LEARNED— WHOSE VALUE IS ONLY THE GREATER BECAUSE, LIKE THE VALUE OF THE STOCK MARKET, IT CAN NEVER ACTUALLY BE TOUCHED OR SEEN.

THE HIGH GEEK-VALUE OF LEARNING ALSO EXPLAINS WHY GEEKS WILL "PAY FOR IT" WITH SUCH LARGE SUMS OF MONEY — CALLING IT THEIR EDUCATION—AND THEN STILL REMEMBER THEIR "ALMA MATER" FONDLY.

THE GEEK BRAIN

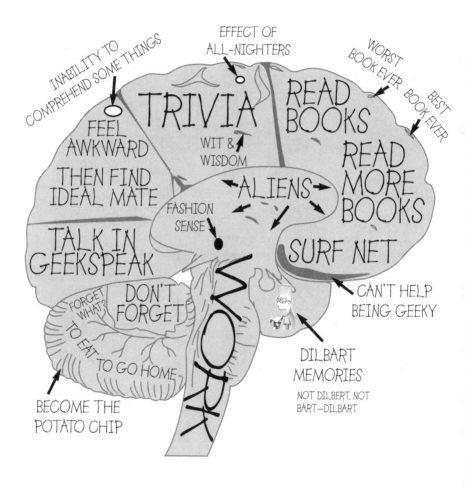

THE "GQ" BASIC QUESTION
#5

DO YOU...
BELIEVE IN "ALIENS"?

THE GEE**X**-FILES

95

GQ #5.1 DO YOU . . .
BELIEVE IN "ALIENS"?

+5

NOT TO WORRY. BELIEVING IN THE EXISTENCE OF "ALIENS"— OR CREATURES LIVING ON A PLANET OTHER THAN THE MOTHER EARTH— ISN'T SOMETHING TO BE ASHAMED OF. PLEASE TAKE THAT BAG OFF YOUR HEAD.

RATHER THAN INDICATING A DYSFUNCTIONAL PARANOID-DELUSION, AS IT SEEMS TO, THE BELIEF HAS ACTUALLY BEEN SHARED BY A LONG LINE OF DISTINGUISHED GEEKS,

GEEKS WHO BELIEVE IN ALIENS— ORSON WELLES, GEORGE LUCAS, AND MICHAEL JACKSON.

WHO ARE ALL QUITE FUNCTIONAL PARANOID-DELUSIONAL.

ONE IS A RINGER. + 1 IF YOU CAN GUESS WHO.

GQ #5.2 DO YOU ...
THINK ABOUT "INTELLIGENT LIFE"? +2
HOPING THERE ARE "MARTIANS"? +3
BUT WILLING TO SETTLE FOR "BACTERIA"? +4

REALLY THINKING ABOUT "INTELLIGENT LIFE" WOULD SEEM TO REQUIRE, FIRST OF ALL, BEING INTELLIGENT LIFE—ON THE THEORY THAT IT TAKES ONE TO THINK ABOUT ONE. BUT THIS LETS OUT A FAIR NUMBER.

SO, AS A WORKAROUND, THE CLASSIC "MARTIAN" WAS MADE UP, SINCE IT REQUIRED NO REAL THOUGHT. THE SIMPLE PICTURE OF A SMALL-BODIED, BULBOUS-HEADED, BUT STILL COINCIDENTALLY PERSON-LIKE, CREATURE BECAME A SYMBOL FOR ALIEN INTELLIGENCE. AND SENSITIVE ANTENNAE STRESSED THE POINT.

WHEN PRESSED, THOUGH, GEEKS WILL ADMIT THAT ALIEN LIFE IS PROBABLY A LOT LESS LIKE A MARTIAN THAN IT IS LIKE "BACTERIA"—UNDERDEVELOPED PHYSIOLOGICALLY, ABLE TO LIVE IN HARSH CONDITIONS, SOCIALLY PRIMITIVE—BUT IN OTHER WORDS STILL A LOT LIKE A GEEK.

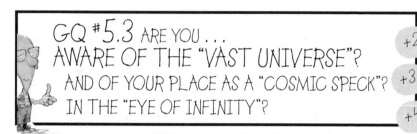

GQ #5.3 ARE YOU . . .
AWARE OF THE "VAST UNIVERSE"?
AND OF YOUR PLACE AS A "COSMIC SPECK"?
IN THE "EYE OF INFINITY"?

+2
+3
+4

GEEKS ARE AWARE OF THE "VAST UNIVERSE" BUT, BECAUSE OF ALL THAT VASTNESS, CAN'T BE AWARE OF MUCH ELSE. SUCH AS BIG GLASS SLIDING DOORS THAT ARE SHUT, OR A LOT OF THINGS THAT PEOPLE TELL THEM LIKE, "LOOK OUT!"

GEEKS ARE ALSO AWARE THAT, IN THIS VAST UNIVERSE, THEY ARE "COSMIC SPECKS." HOWEVER, THEIR EGOS DON'T LIKE THE IDEA ONE BIT, AND KEEP INSISTING ON JUST THE OPPOSITE—THAT

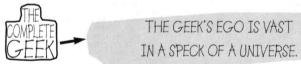

THE GEEK'S EGO IS VAST
IN A SPECK OF A UNIVERSE.

THIS ONLY MAKES THINGS WORSE. BECAUSE THERE ARE ONLY SO MANY TIMES A GEEK CAN RUN INTO THE SAME GLASS DOOR, BEFORE THE EGO HAS TO COMPROMISE. SO, EVENTUALLY, GEEKS AND THEIR EGOS AGREE TO BE SPECKS—BUT PRETTY DAMNED IMPORTANT SPECKS—LIKE SPECKS IN THE "EYE OF INFINITY."

IT IS SURPRISING HOW MANY PEOPLE, IN THEIR ENTIRE LIVES, HAVE NEVER SPOKEN THE LETTERS "UFO." IT JUST NEVER CAME UP. A GEEK, ON THE OTHER HAND, BEGAN UTTERING IT WHEN STILL IN THE CRIB, LOOKING UP AT A STRANGE WHIRLING PHENOMENON (SUBSEQUENTLY IDENTIFIED AS A "MOBILE"). AND AS AN ADULT, EVEN USED SARCASTIC VARIATIONS OF THE LETTERS, SUCH AS "UNBELIEVABLY F____G OBVIOUS."

THE REAL DISTINCTION THAT GEEKS STRIVE FOR, THOUGH, IS TO BE A WITNESS IN A TOP-SECRET GOVERNMENT "INVESTIGATION." TO ACHIEVE THIS GOAL A GEEK SPENDS MANY HOURS SCANNING THE NIGHT SKY FOR TWINKLING LIGHTS, AND OTHER PARANORMAL OCCURRENCES.

KNOWING FULL WELL, OF COURSE, THAT THESE EFFORTS, EVEN IF THEY SUCCEED, MAY WELL BE COVERED UP OR "DENIED" LIKE ALL TOP-SECRET GOVERNMENT INVESTIGATIONS.

ELECTRONIC JOURNAL OF BILL G/

12/31/99 9:05 AM PST
ALIENS HEAD-HUNTING FOR NEW LEADER. UNIVERSE COMES UP EMPTY.
WANT ME.

TELL ALIENS, AM FLATTERED, BUT BUSY. TRANSLATION: MUST BE
KIDDING — NOT WITH EARTH MARKET LIKE IT IS. AM WORTH MORE
THAN ALIEN'S FREQUENT FLYER MILES.

THEN, ALIENS SNEAK-ATTACK — PLAY HOSTAGE-ON-SPACESHIP CARD. AM
FORCED TO IMPROVISE. PLAN A: NEGOTIATE AND WIN. PLAN B: BLOW
SMOKE AND NITPICK. GET MOVING EXPENSES. WILL BE ASTRONOMICAL.

```
ME:     WHY NEED NEW LEADER?
ALIENS: WANT TO SELL "PRODUCT": ALTERNATE REALITY GENERATOR.
        DOES TIME-TRAVEL, VIRTUAL WORLDS, YADDA, YADDA.
        HUMAN VERSION ONLY.
ME:     WHY NOT OTHER LIFE FORMS?
ALIENS: DID MARKET STUDY. HUMANS HAVE MOST DISPOSABLE INCOME
        BY FAR. AND LEADS TO CATCHY NAME: ALTERNATE REALITY
        GENERATOR-HUMAN. ARGH. FOR SHORT. JUST NEED YOU TO...
ME:     GROW MONOPOLY. GOOD CONCEPT. NO ONE DOES BETTER.
ALIENS: BUT...?
ME:     BUT PRODUCT NOT REALISTIC. ON EARTH, ONLY ONE REALITY
        TO MONOPOLIZE. HERE, ALTERNATE REALITIES — AND FICKLE
        CUSTOMERS. MAKES MONOPOLY HARD TO SCHEDULE.
ALIENS: THAT'S WHY NEED YOU. DUH. IF EASY, DO OURSELVES.
ME:     PLAY HARDBALL WITH WRONG BOY, BUG-EYE. EAT LIKES OF
        YOU FOR LUNCH. NOT GOOD LUNCH, EITHER.
```

NEGOTIATION HALTS. AT "SENSITIVE" POINT. SEND FOR MEDIATOR.
MAKE A NOTE: ALIENS TOUCHY ABOUT BUG-EYES.

95

GEEX-FILE #1 DO YOU ...
"WONDER" WHAT LIFE WILL BRING YOU NEXT? +2
TALK "POLITELY" TO STRANGERS AND ALIENS? +3
AND ALWAYS DEFEND "YOUR MOMMA"? +4

I'M JUS SITTIN ON A BENCH ALONGSIDE THE BUS STOP,
WONDERIN WHAT LIFE IS GOIN TO BRING ME NEXT, THE WAY I
ALWAYS LIKE TO DO. WHEN I START TO FEELIN REAL LIGHT IN
THE HEAD.

AS LIGHT AS A FEATHER, IS HOW I FEEL, AN A WHOLE LOT
LIGHTER THAN USUAL, JUS ON ACCOUNT A ME BEIN A IDIOT.
AN THE NEXT THING I KNOW I FIND MYSELF SITTIN ON A
ALIEN SPACESHIP.

DON'T AXE ME HOW I GET THERE. THERE ARE ABOUT SIX
ALIENS WHO ARE ALL SITTIN RIGHT THERE WITH ME, LOOKIN
AT ME WITH THE SAME BUG-EYES BUT AT LEAST THEY ARE
FRIENDLY-LOOKIN. AN THEN THERE'S THIS ONE FELLA I CAN'T
TELL IF HE'S A ALIEN OR NOT, HE'S JUS ALL HEAD. BUT ONE
THING FOR SURE, HE'S NOT FRIENDLY LOOKIN .

SO I FIGURE I SHOULD START WITH HIM. "HAVE WE MET?" I SAY TO HIM, CAUSE THAT'S HOW I LEARNED TO TALK TO STRANGERS.

"NO," HE SAYS, "I'M SURE NOT. I'M BILL. BILL G." AND HE PUTS OUT HIS HAND FOR ME TO SHAKE, SO NOW I KNOW, HE'S A HUMAN BEIN, AN THIS IS JUS AS HUMAN AS HE IS BEIN.

"OK TO MEET YA," I SAY, "I'M FORREST. FORREST GEEK."

AN NOW THIS FELLA BILL LOOKS AT ME REAL INNARESTED. "YOU'RE A GEEK?" HE SAYS.

"YES, I AM." I TELL HIM. "WHY?" I AXE, "YOU KNOW MY MOMMA?" CAUSE I FIGURE, THE ONLY TWO LEF IN THE GEEK FAMILY ARE MOMMA AND ME, AN IT SURE ISN'T ME HE KNOWS. I'M STILL KIND A HALF-THINKIN HE MIGHT BE A ALIEN,

"NO, I'M SURE NOT." HE SAYS AGAIN. AN THIS TIME THE WAY HE SAYS IT, THERE'S A TONE, THAT I DON'T MUCH LIKE HIM TALKIN ABOUT MY MOMMA IN.

GEEX-FILE #2 DO YOU...
HAVE A "REAL KNACK" FOR SOME THINGS?
FEEL LIKE "A IDIOT" WITH OTHERS?
BUT HAVE MORE FUN WITH WHAT YOU "DON'T
KNOW"?

+2

+3

+4

RIGHT THEN THE ALIENS CHIME IN. FROM THE LOOKS OF IT
THEY CAN TALK WITHOUT MOVING THEIR MOUTHS. WHICH IS A
GOOD THING. CAUSE THEY DON'T HAVE MOUTHS. "IF YOU'RE
WONDERING WHY WE BROUGHT YOU HERE..." THEY START TO
SAY, BUT THEN I STOP THEM.

"OH NO, THAT'S NOT NECESSARY," I SAY TO THEM. "IT'S MORE FUN
WHEN I DON'T KNOW."

AN THEN I SEE THE ALIENS ARE STARTIN TO LOOK AT ME THE WAY
EVERYBODY ELSE DOES. MAKIN BUG-EYES LIKE THEY CAN'T
FIGURE ME OUT.

SO I SAY TO THEM, "MAYBE I SHOULD INTRODUCE MYSELF A
LITTLE. LIKE I ALREADY SAID, I'M A GEEK. AN I'M A REAL IDIOT
WHEN IT COMES TO MOST THINGS. AN THEN WITH CERTAIN
OTHER THINGS I HAVE A REAL KNACK FOR THEM. SOME PEOPLE

CALL ME A IDIOT-SAVANT. BUT AS FOR ME, I HAVE A SAYIN, THAT GOES, "A GEEK IS AS A GEEK DOES."

"SO THEN YOU REALLY <u>ARE</u> A GEEK," BILL SAYS.

"YEP, BUT I THINK I ALREADY SAID THAT." I DON'T WANT TO HURT BILL'S FEELINS OR NOTHIN, BUT I THINK I DID.

"WITH AN OPEN MIND," THE ALIENS SAY.

"OH, REAL OPEN, NOW YOU'RE GETTIN THE IDEA," I SAY. NOW THOSE ALIENS IS PRETTY SHARP, EVEN THOUGH THEY DON'T LOOK IT.

THEN BILL AND THE ALIENS START TALKIN ABOUT THIS MACHINE THE ALIENS HAVE. AN I CAN ONLY HEAR CERTAIN THINGS THEY'RE SAYING, LIKE, "HE'S PERFECT" AND "LET'S SEE WHAT HAPPENS IF" AN THEY POINT TO THE MACHINE, SO I FIGURE IT'S THE "WHAT HAPPENS IF" MACHINE.

AN I'M KIND A GLAD I DIDN'T AXE THEM TO EXPLAIN THE WHOLE THING TO ME CAUSE IT SOUNDS A LOT MORE COMPLICATED THAN I COULD A GRAPPED A HOLD A ANYWAY. BUT FINALLY, THEY SAY, "OK, SO IT'S A DEAL."

AN THE NEXT THING I KNOW I'M GETTIN THAT LIGHT-HEADED FEELIN REAL LIGHT IN THE HEAD AGAIN.

ELECTRONIC JOURNAL OF BILL GA

12/31/99 9:25 AM PST

MEDIATOR ARRIVES. REAL GEEK. WHERE DO THESE
GEEKS COME FROM.

CONTINUE NEGOTIATIONS WITH ALIENS — END WITH
SLAM DUNK. ALIENS NO MATCH. WHERE DO THESE
ALIENS COME FROM.

DEAL IS: GENERATE ALTERNATE REALITY.
SUBSTITUTE GEEK FOR ME, LET GEEK MAKE MY
DECISIONS. START WITH LAKEVIEW HIGH. THEN
FIRST SALE TO BIG BLUE. MAJOR CEO DECISIONS.
EVEN BRILLIANT INTERNET STRATEGY.

IF NO DIFFERENCE IN COURSE OF HISTORY. THEN
AGREE TO GO WITH ALIENS. BUT IF ANY
DIFFERENCE AT ALL. GEEK GOES WITH ALIENS.
MAKE A NOTE: OF EXPRESSION ON HIS FACE.

GEEX-FILE #3 ARE YOU ...
PRETTY HANDY WITH "SILLY STUFF"? +2
BUT NOT WITH "GYM"? +2
BECAUSE PHYSICAL FITNESS IS A "LONG-TERM
GOAL"? +3

AN SO NOW I COME TO AN I'M IN A BAGGY SWEAT SUIT AN I'M
WEARIN GLASSES. AN I'M SITTIN IN FRONT OF THIS THING
THAT LOOKS LIKE A TELEVISION, BUT WITHOUT THE
TELEVISION SHOWS.

AN THERE'S SOME YOUNG FELLA STANDIN NEXT TO ME, SAYIN
RIGHT IN MY EAR, "COME ON BILL, GET OFF THE COMPUTER.
GIVE SOMEBODY ELSE A CHANCE."

"BUT I JUST GOT HERE," I TELL HIM, CAUSE MY MOMMA ALWAYS
SAYS TO TELL THE TRUTH.

"YEAH THAT'S WHAT YOU ALWAYS SAY. YOU'RE IMPOSSIBLE!" AN
THEN THE YOUNG FELLA GOES RUNNIN OFF LIKES HE'S REAL
MAD.

SO I FIGURE, AS LONG AS I'M HERE—AN I START PLAYIN AROUND
WITH THE THING. I CAN'T GET IT TO BRING A PICTURE IN, NO

MATTER WHAT I DO, BUT AFTER A WHILE I FIGURE A FEW OTHER THINGS OUT. LIKE IT LOOKS LIKE IT BELONGS TO SOME HIGH SCHOOL, CALLED LAKEVIEW, AN SOMEBODY WAS RIGHT IN THE MIDDLE A PUTTIN TOGETHER THE SCHEDULE FOR THE SCHOOL CLASSES, BEFORE THEY WAS INTERRUPTED.

SO I FIGURE I'LL JUST FINISH IT OFF. THERE'S A WHOLE LOT OF SILLY STUFF I HAVE TO DO, TO MAKE IT WORK, LIKE TYPE IN GOTO THIS AND GOTO THAT ABOUT A MILLION TIMES, AN EVERY ONCE IN A WHILE THE THING TELLS ME I'M MAKIN A "ERROR," BUT IT DOESN'T SAY WHAT A "ERROR" IS. BUT THAT'S OK, CAUSE I'M PRETTY HANDY WITH SILLY STUFF LIKE THAT, BEIN A IDIOT AN ALL.

AN EVENTUALLY IT STARTS WORKIN THE WAY I FIGURE IT SHOULD. AN I EVEN FIND THAT ONE FELLA'S NAME, BILL G.—I NOTICE HE'S A PRETTY SMART FELLA, HE'S GOT GOOD GRADES IN EVERYTHIN EXCEPT GYM. AN SO I THINK, WHAT THE HECK, I'LL DO HIM JUS A LITTLE FAVOR.

RIGHT THEN ANOTHER FELLA COMES IN, THAT LOOKS LIKE A TEACHER, AND SAYS TO ME, "OK, BILL"—SEEMS I'M THE ONLY ONE THAT. CAN'T SEE THE RESEMBLANCE BETWEEN BILL AN ME— "PERIOD'S OVER. YOU'VE GOT TO GO TO YOUR NEXT CLASS.".

"AN WHAT'S THAT SIR?" I AXE HIM, AN I SHOW HIM THE BRAND NEW CLASS SCHEDULE I JUS PRINTED UP.

"UH ... GIRLS' GYM." HE SAYS, AN HE LOOKS AT ME A LITTLE FUNNY WHEN HE SAYS IT.

"WELL THAT'S GOOD," I SAY TO HIM, "I WANT TO BE PHYSICALLY FIT, AS WELL AS GOOD AT FIXIN THIS TV."

AN I'M JUST STARTIN TO WARM UP WITH MY GYM CLASS, WHEN, WOULDN'T YOU KNOW IT, I GET THAT LIGHT-HEADED FEELIN REAL LIGHT IN THE HEAD AGAIN.

GEEX-FILE #4 DO YOU . . .
ALWAYS SAY "OK"?
BECAUSE IT MIGHT "MAKE PEOPLE HAPPY"?
AND LET THEM "WORK OUT THE DETAILS"?

+3
+2
+4

AN THE NEXT THING YOU KNOW I'M SITTIN IN A OFFICE WITH ONE OF THOSE TELEVISIONS AGAIN, BUT NOW THERE ARE A COUPLE OF TELEPHONES, TOO. AN A REAL NICE LADY SITTIN NEXT TO ME.

"BILL," SHE SAYS, LIKE SHE KNOWS ME, "YOU'VE GOT BIG BLUE ON LINE TWO."

"BIG BLUE, WHAT A DOG," I SAY, BECAUSE WHERE I COME FROM BIG BLUE IS THE PRIZE HUNTIN DOG.

"NOW, I KNOW HOW YOU FEEL," THE NICE LADY SAYS TO ME, "BUT YOU'VE GOT TO BE NICE."

SO I PICK UP THE PHONE, AN THERE'S THIS FELLA ON THE LINE ASKIN IF HE CAN BUY SOMETHIN CALLED AN "OPERATIN SYSTEM" FROM ME. WELL I FIGURE I SHOULD BE NICE LIKE THE LADY SAID. SO I TELL HIM, "OK" AN THAT SEEMS TO MAKE HIM HAPPY.

JUST THEN, THE PHONE RINGS ON THE OTHER LINE. AN I PICK THAT ONE UP TOO. IT'S THE FIRST TIME I KNOW WHY GOD GAVE US TWO EARS, AN IT TURNS OUT THERE'S A FELLA ON THAT LINE THAT SAYS HE WANTS TO SELL ME AN "OPERATIN SYSTEM."

SO I SAY "OK" TO HIM, TOO. IT'S REALLY SOMETHIN HOW HAPPY YOU CAN MAKE PEOPLE, JUST BY SAYIN OK TO THEM.

AN THEN I PUT THE TWO PHONES TOGETHER, AN I JUS LET THE TWO OF THEM WORK OUT THE DETAILS.

GEEX-FILE #5 CAN YOU . . .
"ANSWER" ANY QUESTION?
WITHOUT "LOOKING STUPID"?
SUCH AS, SHOULD WE WORK ON THE "ENTER-NIT"?

+2
-
+4
+3

AFTER THAT, I START GETTIN LIGHT-HEADED, AND COMIN TO, AND GETTIN LIGHT-HEADED AN COMIN TO. AN EVERYTIME I COME TO, SOMEBODY'LL ASK ME A QUESTION THAT I HAVE TO TO GIVE AN ANSWER TO.

LIKE "BILL SHOULD WE COPY THE OTHER PRODUCT, OR START FROM SCRATCH?"

AN I SAY, "COPY," BECAUSE COPYIN IS ONE THING THAT EVEN A IDIOT KNOWS IS GOIN TO WORK PRETTY GOOD,

AN ANOTHER TIME, SOMEBODY WILL SAY, "BILL, SHOULD WE SELL REAL EXPENSIVE, OR REAL CHEAP," AN I SAY "REAL CHEAP." BECAUSE I FIGURE, WE ONLY COPIED THE THING, WE SURE CAN'T SELL IT FOR EXPENSIVE.

BUT MOST OF THE TIME I JUST SAY WHAT MAKES PEOPLE HAPPY. I JUST SAY "OK." OR I SAY"DO WHAT YOU THINK IS BEST." AN SURE ENOUGH EVERYBODY IS REAL HAPPY, AN WORKS REAL HARD.

AN EVERYTIME I COME TO, THERE'S SOMETHIN NEW AN DIFFERENT, EITHER THE OFFICE WHERE I'M IN KEEPS GETTIN

BIGGER. OR THERE'S MORE PEOPLE RUNNIN AROUND. AN
PRETTY SOON EVERYTHIN IS NEW AN DIFFERENT, EXCEPT
MY OUTFIT.

AN THEY EVEN PUT A LITTLE SIGN ON MY OFFICE THAT SAYS
"CEO." AT FIRST I DON'T KNOW WHAT THAT IS. BUT THEN I
FIGURE OUT—FROM HOW EVERYBODY IS TELLIN ME WHAT A
GOOD JOB I'M DOIN, AND HOW I'M THE SMARTEST PERSON
THEY EVER MET—A CEO IS ONE A THOSE JOBS, LIKE BEIN A
LIFEGUARD, WHERE ALL YOU HAVE TO DO IS TAKE THE CREDIT
CAUSE NOBODY'S DROWNIN YET.

AN THE ONLY PROBLEM I SEEM TO HAVE IS, I'M NOT TOO
GOOD AT TALKIN TO THE PRESS. AN EVERYTIME I DO, IT
ALWAYS ENDS UP WITH I SAY SOMETHIN EMBARRASSIN. AN
THEN, EVERYBODY SAYS TO ME, "WHY'D YOU SAY THAT, BILL,
YOU SOUNDED LIKE A IDIOT?" SO I JUS DON'T DO MUCH TALKIN
TO THE PRESS.

AN THE VERY LAST TIME I REMEMBER COMIN TO, SOMEBODY
SAYS TO ME, "BILL SHOULD WE WORK ON ..." AN WHAT THEY SAY
AFTER THAT I'M NOT TOO SURE OF EXACTLY, BUT IT SOUNDS
LIKE "THE ENTER NIT." NOW I NEVER HEARD OF "THE ENTER
NIT," TO BE HONEST WITH YOU, BUT IT SOUNDS LIKE A GOOD
IDEA. LIKE SOMETHIN THAT GIVES EVERY NIT-WIT AN IDIOT
LIKE ME A FAIR CHANCE TO ENTER. SO I SAY "OK." AN NOBODY
SEEMS TO THINK I'M STUPID FOR SAYIN IT, WHICH IS ALL I
CARE ABOUT.

GEEX-FILE #6 DO YOU . . .
WANT TO MAKE "A DIFFERENCE"?
AT LEAST IN THE "LITTLE THINGS"?
AND WISH PEOPLE WOULDN'T WORRY SO MUCH
ABOUT " RHYTHM"?

+2

+4

+2

AN THEN, BEFORE I KNOW IT, I FIND MYSELF COMIN TO, BACK UP
ON THE ALIEN SPACESHIP AGAIN. AN THE ALIENS ARE ALL
STILL HUDDLED AROUND THAT SAME "WHAT HAPPENS IF"
MACHINE, BUT NOW THEY'RE KIND A YUCKIN IT UP, WHICH THEY
CAN DO EVEN WITHOUT HAVIN MOUTHS.

AN BILL G, HE'S THERE TOO, BUT NOT LOOKIN ANY TOO HAPPY.

SO I SAY TO HIM, "WHAT'S THE MATTER BILL? I GOT YOU INTO
THE GIRL'S GYM CLASS."

AN HE SAYS, "MY WHOLE LIFE, IT'S MEANINGLESS. IF I NEVER
EXISTED, IT WOULDN'T HAVE MADE ONE BIT OF DIFFERENCE."

AN NOW I SEE WHAT HE'S SAD ABOUT. HE'S PICTURIN HIMSELF AS
JIMMY STEWART IN "IT'S A WONNERFUL LIFE" AN IT IS THE
HOLIDAYS AN ALL.

AN I FEEL SO BAD FOR HIM, SO I SAY, "LOOK IT BILL, IT DOESN'T MATTER ABOUT ALL THAT 'WHAT HAPPENS IF' STUFF. CERTAIN THINGS ARE GOIN TO HAPPEN THE WAY THEY HAPPEN NO MATTER WHAT. THE BEST YOU CAN HOPE FOR IS THAT YOU GET OUT A THE WAY. THE ONLY THINGS THAT REALLY MATTER , WHERE YOU REALLY MAKE A DIFFERENCE, ARE WITH THE LITTLE THINGS."

"SUCH AS?" HE SAYS. AN HE'S STILL KIND A GOT THAT TONE THAT I DON'T MUCH LIKE. BUT I FIGURE, WHAT THE HECK, IT'S NEW YEAR'S EVE.

"SUCH AS DANCIN, FOR INSTANCE." I TELL HIM.

"DANCING? I DON'T DANCE." AN IF YOU LOOK AT HIM, YOU WOULDN'T BE TOO SURPRISED.

"WELL, MAYBE YOU SHOULD BILL. MAYBE WE ALL SHOULD." AN THEN I GET A IDEA, WHICH COME TO THINK OF IT, IS SOMETHIN OF A FIRST FOR ME.

AN SO I AXE THE ALIENS TO HAVE A LOOK AT THAT "WHAT HAPPENS IF" MACHINE A THEIRS FOR TWO SECONDS. AN THEY LET ME LOOK AT IT. I GUESS THEY FIGURE A IDIOT LIKE ME CAN'T DO NO HARM. AN I START TO PLAY WITH IT A LITTLE—

109

IT'S KIND A LIKE A TELEVISION SHOW, WITHOUT THE TELEVISION.
AN BEFORE TOO LONG I FIX IT UP JUS FINE.

AN THEN YOU CAN PROBABLY GUESS WHAT HAPPENS NEXT.
I GET BILL AN ALL THOSE ALIENS DOIN A LATIN-BEAT LINE DANCE
RIGHT OUT A THEIR SPACESHIP, OR AT LEAST THEY ARE TRYING TO.
TURNS OUT ALIENS DON'T HAVE ANY RHYTHM. NEITHER DOES BILL.
BUT IN MY "WHAT HAPPENS IF" NOBODY REALLY WORRIES ABOUT IT
ALL THAT MUCH.

GEEX-FILE #7 DO YOU . . .
"DO" A LATIN-BEAT LINE DANCE?
WITHOUT THE "LATIN-BEAT" OR THE "LINE"?
    AND JUST CALL IT "DANCE"?
+2
+3
+4

NOT "EVERYONE" CAN LEARN THE MACARENA

9:45 AM PST DECEMBER 31, 1999

BILL WHERE HAVE YOU BEEN? I WAS WORRIED.

BILL...
ARE YOU ALRIGHT?

UNNATURAL GESTURES. BLANK STARE. UNABLE TO COMMUNICATE.— MUST ANALYZE...

EITHER YOU'RE DANCING OR ALIENS HAVE DONE THIS TO YOU.

Have you ever heard of the Macarena?

THE "GQ" BASIC QUESTION
#4
ARE YOU...ALIENATED BY "SOCIAL CONVENTIONS"?

HOW TO LOSE FRIENDS BUT INFLUENCE GEEKS
BY DALE CARNEGEEK

115

ELECTRONIC JOURNAL OF BILL G/

12/31/99 6:58 PM PST

MAKE A NOTE: NO MORE GOLF WITH LAME DUCK PRESIDENTS.

WASTED WHOLE AFTERNOON WITH SMALL TALK. WHAT THINK OF WEATHER. HOLD CLUB LIKE THIS. HOW ABOUT THOSE JAPANESE.

NO DISCUSSION OF BASIC PROGRAMMING OR ANTI-TRUST. AS IF HAVE NOTHING BETTER TO DO.

SECRET SERVICE HAS MORE DEPTH. AT LEAST THEY DON'T TALK TOO MUCH.

LONGEST 18 HOLES SINCE GOPHER GOT LOOSE ON ESTATE. NOTHING WORSE THAN GOLF WITH BUBBA'S.

MR. PRESIDENT! YOU LOOK WORRIED IS IT THE MILLENNIUM?

YES. I WON'T HAVE A JOB. AND I DON'T KNOW HOW I'LL DO IN THE REAL WORLD.

YOU MEAN, MORE GOLF WITH BILL G.?

THE LAST TIME WAS A DISASTER. I TRIED EVERYTHING IN THE BOOK—IN YOUR BOOK, DALE—BUT I COULDN'T BOND ONE TINY BIT WITH A GEEK LIKE HIM. AND I <u>PRIDE</u> MYSELF ON MY BONDING SKILLS.

DON'T FEEL BAD, I'VE BEEN HAVING TROUBLE MYSELF.

TAKING A BEATING ON YOUR MONEY-BACK GUARANTEE?

THAT'S NOT WHY YOU'RE HERE IS IT?

NO. YOUR BOOK IS THE REASON I'M PRESIDENT. BUT WHAT AM I GOING TO DO IN THE REAL WORLD, WITH ALL THESE GEEKS LIKE BILL?

I'VE GOT A NEW SEMINAR IT'S CALLED—THE 13 RULES OF HOW TO LOSE FRIENDS, BUT INFLUENCE GEEKS.

GEE, DO I HAVE TO LOSE MY FRIENDS?

WELL, NO. IT'S YOUR CHOICE, BUT . . .

OH . . . OK. THEY'RE ALL INCARCERATED ANYWAY.

RULE #1 DO YOU ...
ALLOCATE YOUR "TIME RESOURCES"? +2
IN A WAY THAT MAKES "SUNDAY CHURCH" INEFFICIENT? +2
BUT A VIRTUAL DATE SEEM "ATTRACTIVE"? +4

THE FIRST THING YOU'VE GOT TO DO IS

PICK SOMETHING THAT BILL LIKES TO DO. THIS IS HARDER
THAN IT SOUNDS—IT HAS TO BE A GOOD ALLOCATION OF HIS
PRECIOUS TIME.

CAN YOU GIVE ME AN EXAMPLE?

WELL, CHURCH, FOR EXAMPLE—THAT'S INEFFICIENT. BILL FEELS
HE'S GOT BETTER THINGS TO DO.

OK I SEE WHAT YOU MEAN. IF HE HAS TO CHOOSE BETWEEN A
DRIVE IN HIS PORSCHE AND BEGGING FOR FORGIVENESS ...

BUT A VIRTUAL DATE,
ON THE INTERNET—
BILL G. WOULD LIKE
THAT

NO. I DON'T NEED
ANY MORE TROUBLE
WITH HILLARY..

SO THEN IT LOOKS LIKE GOLF AGAIN.

BUT WHAT SHOULD I DO DIFFERENTLY THIS TIME?

117

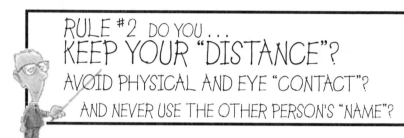

RULE #2 DO YOU...
KEEP YOUR "DISTANCE"?
AVOID PHYSICAL AND EYE "CONTACT"?
AND NEVER USE THE OTHER PERSON'S "NAME"?

+2
+2
+4

WELL, WHY DON'T YOU JUST STICK A FORK IN ME AND CALL ME FINISHED. THOSE ARE ALL THE THINGS I MAKE MY LIVING ON.

LET ME ASK YOU MR. PRESIDENT, IS IT A GOOD LIVING?

WHAT HAVE YOU BEEN LOOKING AT? THOSE ARE CONFIDENTIAL FILES!

NOW, MR. PRESIDENT, I'M JUST ASKING. ANYWAY, THERE ARE CERTAIN THINGS TO AVOID WITH GEEKS, SUCH AS PHYSICAL CONTACT AND EYE CONTACT. HERE ARE SOME ILLUSTRATIONS—THE GEEKS' TWO NIGHTMARES—THAT EXPLAIN WHY.

BUT WHY DOESN'T BILL G. USE THE OTHER PERSON'S NAME?

IT WAS IN MY FIRST BOOK. GEEKS CONSIDER MY FIRST BOOK TO BE "SUCKING UP."

THEN I MUST BE ONE GOD-AWFUL...

SUCK-UP, SEE, THIS IS WORKING.

THE GEEK'S NIGHTMARE #1

BAXTERIA, AND YOU ARE?

THE GEEK'S NIGHTMARE #2

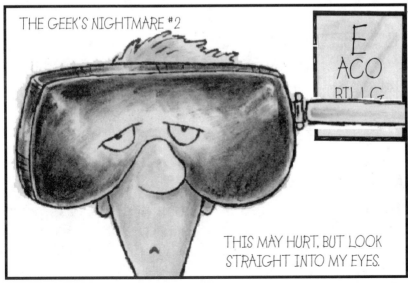

THIS MAY HURT, BUT LOOK
STRAIGHT INTO MY EYES.

RULE #3 DO YOU . . .
"ROCK"—BUT DON'T ROLL?
AS IF YOU WERE RIDING A "ROCKING HORSE"?
AND SURROUND YOURSELF WITH PEOPLE "WHO ROCK"?

+2

+1

+6

OH, SO THAT'S WHAT HE KEPT DOING—ROCKING BACK AND FORTH, BACK AND FORTH, WITH HIS ARMS FOLDED— EVERY TIME I WAS TRYING TO LINE UP A PUTT. IT WAS DISTRACTING AS HELL.

BUT YOU'RE SUPPOSED TO DO IT TOO. HE THINKS IT MEANS YOU HAVE DEPTH, LIKE HIM. AND REMEMBER DO IT EXACTLY THE SAME WAY AS HE DOES—DON'T PUT ANY RHYTHM INTO IT.

WELL, THE VICE PRESIDENT CAN GIVE ME LESSONS THERE, BUT WHAT'S THE POINT OF IT?

BILL G. SAYS IT HELPS HIM TO CONCENTRATE. BUT ALSO—IT BEATS YOUR OTHER ALTERNATIVE: "EX-PRESIDENT UNOFFICIAL FOREIGN POLICY ADVISOR."

WHICH IS A PRETTY CROWDED JOB MARKET.

JUST MAKE SURE EVERYBODY ON YOUR STAFF WHO MEETS BILL ROCKS , TOO.

THE SECRET SERVICE AGENTS? I CAN'T EVEN GET THOSE GUYS TO DO SIMPLE THINGS, LIKE NOT TELL WHEN I LEAVE THE WHITE HOUSE LATE AT NIGHT.

RULE #4 DO YOU ...
NOT CARE ABOUT PHONY "SMALL TALK"? +2
NEVER SHOW MORE THAN A "FLICKER OF EMOTION"? +4
BUT CRACK UP OVER THE "TELEPHONE BOOTH" +4
PRANK?

LET'S GO OVER ALL THE THINGS YOU DID

THE LAST TIME YOU WENT GOLFING WITH BILL G. THAT CAUSED ALL THE TROUBLE. FIRST OF ALL, YOU SHOULDN'T HAVE MADE SMALL TALK ABOUT HIS PERSONAL LIFE. BILL G. THINKS THAT'S PHONY. BESIDES, HE DOESN'T HAVE ONE.

OH YES HE DOES, DALE. MY STAFF DUG IT UP. IT TOOK THEM A COUPLE OF WEEKS, BUT THEY FINALLY FOUND IT IN WITH SOME BOXES OF PAPERS IN HILLARY'S OFFICE.

OK, BUT WHAT HAPPENED? YOU KNEW HIS MOTHER HAD JUST DIED, AND SO ... YOU TRIED TO SHARE WITH HIM THE PAIN OF YOUR MOTHER'S DEATH. RIGHT? AND DID IT WORK?

EMOTIONALLY, YOU MEAN? DALE—NOTHING. I HAVEN'T BEEN SHUT OUT LIKE THAT, WELL, NOT SINCE PAULA JONES.

BUT DID YOU NOTICE THE "FLICKER"?

ON THE 3RD HOLE, I THOUGHT THE CHIMICHANGA HE HAD FOR LUNCH KIND OF REPEATED ON HIM.

NO, THAT WAS THE "FLICKER OF EMOTION." AND IF YOU USE THE "TELEPHONE BOOTH" PRANK—THAT'S WHEN YOU PASS A PAY PHONE, AND YOU RUN IN AND CHECK THE COIN SLOT FOR LOOSE CHANGE—THEN YOU GET THE "FLICKER OF HUMOR."

LIKE A PHILLY CHEESESTEAK. BY THE WAY, DALE, I'M GETTING HUNGRY. DO GEEK SEMINARS HAVE BUFFETS?

121

RULE #5 DO YOU ...
NOT CARE ABOUT PHONY GOLFING "TIPS"? +2
NEVER GIVE STROKES, ONLY "UNDO'S"? +2
AND ALWAYS DRILL DOWN, TAKE CHARGE AND +5
"DRIVE THE CART"?

WHEN YOU GO GOLFING WITH BILL G

YOU SHOULDN'T GIVE HIM ANY TIPS ABOUT HIS GOLF GAME. BILL G. THINKS THAT'S PHONY, TOO.

BESIDES, HE DOESN'T HAVE ONE. I KNOW, WE SPENT THE WHOLE DAY LOOKING FOR IT. WHAT ABOUT MULLIGANS?

NO. CALL THEM UNDO'S—AND ONE MORE THING, MR. PRESIDENT. BILL G. LIKES TO DRILL DOWN, TAKE CHARGE.

YOU DON'T MEAN ...

YOU HAVE TO LET HIM DRIVE THE CART.

I WON'T DO IT. THAT'S AN INSULT TO MY OFFICE! THE COMMANDER-IN-CHIEF ALWAYS DRIVES THE CART.

"YOUR OFFICE" HAS MORE CHECKS AND BALANCES THAN AN ARKANSAS BANKER.

WHILE BILL'S GOT THE ENTIRE FREE WORLD BY THE NASTIES

I FEEL THEIR PAIN.

JUST WAIT. IT GETS WORSE. THEN THIS DOESN'T SEEM SO BAD

RULE #6 DO YOU ...
WISH WHOEVER IS TALKING WOULD JUST "HURRY UP"? +2
SO YOU WOULDN'T "HAVE TO INTERRUPT" WHAT
THEY'RE COMING TO IN A MOMENT? +2
TO INSIST THEY TALK ABOUT IT "NOW"? +2

THE BASIC IDEA HERE IS, WHEN YOU'RE TALKING TO BILL G. YOU SHOULD TALK FASTER.

HOW FAST SHOULD I TALK?

FASTER THAN YOU'RE TALKING.

YOUMEANLIKETHIS?

THAT'S GOOD. BUT THEN ONCE YOU'RE TALKING LIKE THAT, YOU'LL NEED TO PICK IT UP A LITTLE MORE . THE RULE IS, HOWEVER FAST YOU HAPPEN TO BE TALKING, TALK A LITTLE FASTER THAN THAT.

YOU MEAN LIKE WHEN I'M TALKING TO HILLARY, ABOUT WHERE I WAS THE NIGHT BEFORE?

YES, EXCEPT BILL NEVER CHANGES HIS HAIRSTYLE. THE IDEA IS, BILL G. WANTS TO MAKE YOU FEEL LIKE HE'S ONE STEP AHEAD OF YOU. BUT YOU CAN BEAT HIM AT HIS OWN GAME, IF YOU JUST TALK FASTER.

BUT WHAT DOES BILL SAY WHEN I'M TALKING SO FAST I DON'T KNOW WHAT I'M TALKING ABOUT?

I DON'T KNOW, SIR ... WHAT DO THE AMERICAN PEOPLE USUALLY SAY?

123

RULE #7 DO YOU ...
"PEPPER" WITH QUESTIONS?
UNTIL IT SEEMS POINTLESS TO "GO ON"?
AND CALL THAT "THE HEART OF THE MATTER"?

+2

+4

+4

THE NEXT THING BILL G. LIKES TO DO,
ONCE HE HAS YOU TALKING REAL FAST, IS PEPPER YOU.

LIKE IN BASEBALL?

NO, LIKE IN DEAD MEAT. HE ASKS YOU QUESTION AFTER QUESTION,
AND IT DOESN'T MATTER HOW WELL PREPARED YOU ARE, AT SOME
POINT HE'LL ASK YOU ONE WHERE THERE'S ONLY ONE ANSWER.

AND THAT'S, "WHAT'S THE POINT?"

HOW DID YOU KNOW?

IT SOUNDS LIKE A PRESS CONFERENCE. YOU TAKE ENOUGH
QUESTIONS, YOU GET TO WHERE THEY HAVE TO LEAD YOU OFF THE
STAGE, I ALWAYS FEEL LIKE I JUST WON BEST PIG OF SHOW.

BUT THAT'S WHEN YOU CAN IMPRESS BILL G. THE MOST.

YOU'RE KIDDING, HE'S INTO LIVESTOCK ?

NO, HE'S INTO WINNING. YOU HAVE TO TELL HIM WHAT A GREAT
QUESTION HE JUST CAME UP WITH. AND HOW YOU'LL LOOK INTO
THAT RIGHT AWAY.

DALE, I WAS JUST THINKING—WHAT IF I SLIP UP AND CALL HIM
COKIE?

RULE #8 DO YOU ...
"ALWAYS" ARGUE OR DEBATE?
FOR THE SAKE OF THE "INTELLECTUAL" CHALLENGE?
NOT FOR THE SAKE OF BEING "A BORE"?

+3
+2
+4

A BONDING EXPERIENCE WITH BILL G.–

A) YOU KEEP TALKING FASTER AND FASTER WHILE BILL PRETENDS HE'S BORED

B) BILL STARTS PEPPERING YOU WITH QUESTIONS WHILE YOU PRETEND YOU'RE NOT BORED..

BILL CALLS THIS BEING "INTELLECTUALLY" CHALLENGED

SOUNDS LIKE AN ENTITLEMENT PROGRAM FOR THE WELL-EDUCATED?

IT'S HOW YOU KEEP BILL FROM BEING BORED. YOU HAVE TO ARGUE AND DEBATE. THIS IS THE TIME TO LET OUT ANY UNFLATTERING INSTINCTS.

I HAVE A SECRET CRAVING FOR FRIED FOOD. WILL THAT HELP ME ?

NO, BILL'S INTO INDIAN. BUT THE BASIC IDEA IS, BILL CALLS HIS OWN IDEAS, "REALLY NEAT" "SUPERFUN" AND "HARDCORE." AND THEN HE CALLS YOUR IDEAS "REALLY DUMB" "CRUMMY" AND "RANDOM TO THE MAX." INTELLECTUAL CHALLENGE ISN'T AS HARD AS IT SOUNDS.

AND THE GOAL IS ...?

YOU HAVE TO BE A BORE, SO YOU WON'T BE BORING.

SO IT'S LIKE BEING A PRESIDENT, WITHOUT BEING PRESIDENTIAL. PIECE OF CAKE, RIGHT OVER THERE ... DALE, DO YOU WANT THAT?

125

RULE #9 ARE YOU . . .
"PRETTY SURE" YOU'RE ALWAYS RIGHT? +3
BECAUSE OF YOUR "IQ"? +3
AND PRETTY SURE OF YOUR IQ, BECAUSE YOU'RE +6
"ALWAYS RIGHT"?

THE KEY TO THIS ONE IS THAT BILL G. ALWAYS THINKS HE'S RIGHT BECAUSE OF HIS IQ.

SO HE'S HAD HIS IQ TESTED?

NO, YOU'RE THINKING OF THE LAST RULE—SOMETIMES YOU TEST HIS PATIENCE, BUT HIS IQ IS WHAT HE CALLS A "GIVEN."

WHAT DOES HE MEAN A "GIVEN"?

HE MEANS IT'S AN IDEA THAT'S "GIVEN" TO HIM BY THE PEOPLE AROUND HIM, WHO ALWAYS SAY HOW HE'S THE SMARTEST PERSON THEY'VE EVER MET.

YOU MEAN, THAT'S ALL I HAVE TO DO?—IS SAY HOW "HE'S THE SMARTEST PERSON I EVER MET"? THAT'S TOO EASY!

YOU SAY THAT NOW. BUT WAIT UNTIL THE WORDS HAVE TO COME OUT OF YOUR MOUTH..

COME ON, DALE, I'M A CAREER POLITICIAN. GIVE ME A LITTLE CREDIT.

RULE #10 DO YOU...
"REPEAT" AN OPPOSING ARGUMENT? **+1**
IN A SARCASTIC TONE— THEN "LOSE YOUR TEMPER"? **+3**
AND YELL "THAT'S THE STUPIDEST THING I'VE
EVER HEARD"? **+5**

OK, MR. PRESIDENT, FOR THIS ONE WE'RE GOING TO HAVE TO DO A LITTLE EXERCISE.

GOOD, LET'S CALL SOME PHOTOGRAPHERS. IT'LL HELP MY IMAGE.

NOT THAT KIND OF EXERCISE, SIR. WHAT WE'RE GOING TO DO IS, I'LL SAY A SIMPLE ARGUMENT, LIKE, "YOU CAN'T FIT A SQUARE PEG IN A ROUND HOLE," AND THEN YOU REPEAT IT BACK, SARCASTICALLY. LIKE, "YOU <u>CAN'T</u> FIT A <u>SQUARE</u> <u>PEG</u> IN A <u>ROUND</u> <u>HOLE</u>??!!"

OK, OK. IT'S LIKE THE DEBATES, WHERE I SAY "<u>LEADERSHIP</u> REQUIRES <u>CHARACTER</u>?"

LET'S START. | OK, COMPUTERS ARE HARD TO USE.

EASY— <u>COMPUTERS</u> ARE <u>HARD</u> TO <u>USE</u>??!! | GOOD— GEEKS NEVER HAVE ANY FUN.

THAT'S HARDER— <u>GEEKS</u> NEVER <u>HAVE</u> ANY <u>FUN</u>??!! | GOOD, NOW... BILL G. IS A MEGALO-MANIAC.

127

KEEP GOING! NEXT, YOU LOSE YOUR TEMPER, AND THEN YOU YELL, JUST LIKE BILL G. ALWAYS DOES, "THAT'S THE STUPIDEST THING I'VE EVER HEARD."

THERE'S NO WAY, DALE, I'VE BEEN LISTENING TO CONGRESS FOR EIGHT YEARS. I'VE TOTALLY LOST MY STUPID-BEARINGS.

YOU'VE GOT TO PUSH YOURSELF! COME ON, GET MAD! ... FEEL THE BURN!

OK, OK, JUST LET ME THINK OF SOMETHING REALLY STUPID ... GOT IT, OK ... THAT'S THE STUPIDEST THING I'VE EVER HEARD!!!

WHOA, VERY CONVINCING. WHAT WERE YOU THINKING?

THAT BILL G. RAN FOR PRESIDENT, AND I HAD TO VOTE FOR NEWT.

RULE #11 DO YOU ...
"MAKE" NO APOLOGIES?   +2
USE OBSCENITY WHEN YOU MEAN "SORRY"?   +3
AND SEND "A FLAME" LATE AT NIGHT, THAT HELPS
YOU GET TO SLEEP?   +4

OK, MR. PRESIDENT, DON'T TAKE THIS THE WRONG WAY, BUT YOU
REMEMBER THE TIME, WHEN YOU WERE RUNNING IN THE NEW
HAMPSHIRE PRIMARY, AND IT CAME OUT THAT ...

THAT I WAS CHEATING ON HILLARY IN THE HALLWAY OF THE
GOVERNOR'S MANSION WITH A FLOOZY NIGHT-CLUB SINGER? NO
DALE, I HAD A FRONTAL LOBOTOMY, AND I COMPLETELY FORGOT.

WELL, TRY TO REMEMBER. BECAUSE WHAT YOU DID NEXT IS YOU
WENT ON TELEVISION, AND YOU APOLOGIZED TO THE AMERICAN
PUBLIC, AND THE PUBLIC FORGAVE YOU, AND THEN YOU WENT ON
TO BE PRESIDENT.

AND NOW I'M LOOKING FOR A JOB AGAIN. WHAT ARE YOU SAYING,
THAT I HAVE TO HUMILIATE MYSELF IN PUBLIC ALL OVER AGAIN?

NO WHAT I'M SAYING IS, THAT ALL HAPPENED A LONG TIME AGO.
BUT IT WOULDN'T HAPPEN LIKE THAT NOW, NOT WITH SO MANY
GEEKS LIKE BILL G. AROUND. SEE, BILL DOESN'T APOLOGIZE—AND
HE DOESN'T ACCEPT APOLOGIES, ESPECIALLY NOT ONES THAT
ARE OBVIOUSLY ...

YES I KNOW, OBVIOUSLY. BUT WHAT DOES HE DO, INSTEAD?

WELL, HERE'S WHAT BILL WOULD DO. HE WOULD "MAKE NO APOLOGIES." NOT THAT HE WOULDN'T FEEL SORRY, SOMEWHERE DEEP DOWN HE MIGHT, BUT EVERY TIME HE FELT LIKE HE WAS ABOUT TO SAY THE WORD, "SORRY"—BEFORE IT CAME OUT OF HIS MOUTH—HE WOULD JUST SUBSTITUTE A FOUR-LETTER WORD STARTING WITH THE SIXTH LETTER OF THE ALPHABET.

GEEZ, HOW DOES HE COUNT THAT FAST?

AND THEN TO REALLY SETTLE MATTERS, HE WOULD START A FLAME WAR ON THE INTERNET. THAT'S WHERE LATE AT NIGHT, BILL G. SENDS OUT A REALLY INSULTING E-MAIL, THAT GETS EVERYBODY FLAMING MAD, AND THEN EVERYBODY ON THE INTERNET STARTS FLAMING HIM BACK, AND THEN FLAMING EACH OTHER, AND PRETTY SOON NOBODY REMEMBERS WHAT STARTED THE WHOLE THING ANYWAY.

AND WHAT HAPPENS TO BILL G.?

THE WHOLE THING HELPS HIM TO UNWIND. SO BY NOW HE'S SLEEPING THE SLEEP OF BABES.

THAT LAST PART I DON'T BELIEVE. GEEKS NEVER GET TO SLEEP WITH BABES.

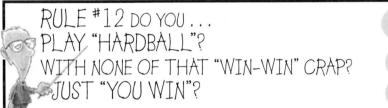

RULE #12 DO YOU . . .
PLAY "HARDBALL"?
WITH NONE OF THAT "WIN-WIN" CRAP?
JUST "YOU WIN"?

+3

+3

+3

BILL G. ALWAYS PLAYS HARDBALL. THAT MEANS HE ALWAYS WINS. AND WHEN HE WINS, EVERYBODY ELSE LOSES. HE DOESN'T GO FOR ANY OF THAT WIN-WIN CRAP.

BUT WHAT ABOUT WHEN HE LOSES, WOULDN'T HE BE BETTER OFF WITH A WIN-WIN INSTEAD?

CAN'T HAPPEN—BILL NEVER LOSES. HIS STRATEGY IS—"LOSING" JUST MEANS IT'S TAKING HIM LONGER TO WIN.

WELL, WHAT ABOUT WHEN HE'S LOSING FOR A LONG TIME?

OH, HE'S GOT A LOT OF PATIENCE. WHAT HAPPENED IN YOUR GOLF MATCH?

I WAS 24 STROKES AHEAD .

AND THEN?

I 26 PUTTED THE 18TH.

WAS BILL PATIENT?

YEAH, THE WHOLE TIME HE JUST KEPT STAMPING HIS FEET, AND CRYING, "I ALWAYS WIN!"

131

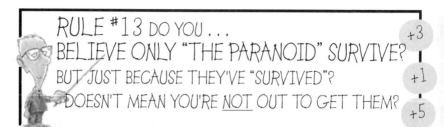

RULE #13 DO YOU . . .
BELIEVE ONLY "THE PARANOID" SURVIVE? +3
BUT JUST BECAUSE THEY'VE "SURVIVED"? +1
DOESN'T MEAN YOU'RE NOT OUT TO GET THEM? +5

BILL G. STILL FACES A SERIOUS THREAT FROM COMPETITION.

YOU MEAN CUBA COMPUTA, AND VIETNAM RAM?

NO. COMPETITORS HERE IN THE U. S. WHO REMAIN . . . ANONYMOUS,

ANONYMOUS. HOW CAN THAT...

QUIET! WE NEED TO BE DISCREET.

OK, BUT HOW CAN THAT BE?

HOW CAN YOU BE DISCREET?

NO, HOW CAN COMPANIES BE ANONYMOUS?

OH, IT ALL STARTED AS

BILL'S FEW REMAINING COMPETITORS BANDED TOGETHER A FEW YEARS AGO TO REPORT HIM TO THE JUSTICE DEPARTMENT—FOR ANTI-TRUST VIOLATIONS.

YES, I REMEMBER THAT. THEY DID IT ANONYMOUSLY, SO BILL G. WOULDN'T FIND OUT THEY WERE TELLING ON HIM.

WELL, HE FOUND OUT.

HOW—DID BILL G. HACK INTO THE JUSTICE DEPARTMENT COMPUTERS?

NO, PROCESS OF ELIMINATION. AND AFTER THAT, HE RECRIMINATED, RUTHLESSLY—HE SUCKED THEIR SMARTEST GEEKS RIGHT OUT OF THEM. AND IT JUST KIND OF SNOWBALLED. UNTIL ...

THE ENTIRE COMPANIES HAD TO GO INTO HIDING. BUT DALE, ISN'T THAT BAD FOR THEIR BUSINESS?

THE UNDERGROUND ECONOMY, MR. PRESIDENT. IT'S THRIVING.

WHAT ABOUT THE EMPLOYEES?

THEY'RE COVERED, UNDER THE WITNESS PROTECTION PLAN.

THIS EXPLAINS THE REPORTS WE'VE BEEN GETTING. MORE ANTI-TRUST PROBLEMS?

NO UNREPORTED INCOME

WE'RE BEING TIPPED OFF BY SOMEONE NAMED BILL G.

CONCLUSION–DO YOU . . .
REMAIN "CHILD-LIKE"?
WITH CERTAIN CHILD-LIKE "WAYS"?
THAT NO ONE REALLY "LIKED IN YOU" AS A CHILD?

+6

+4

+2

IN CONCLUSION, A FEW PERSONAL OBSERVATIONS ABOUT
BILL G.–

WHEN YOU FIRST MEET BILL G. THE FIRST THING YOU NOTICE
ABOUT HIM IS, HE SEEMS TO BE MORE A CHILD THAN A MAN. IT'S
PARTLY THE WAY HE LOOKS, THE WAY HE HAS THIS DOWNY
FACIAL HAIR, AND YOU CAN TELL HE DOESN'T NEED TO SHAVE, AND
THE WAY HIS CHIN STILL HASN'T COME AROUND TO THE POINT
OF WHERE YOU WOULD ACTUALLY CALL IT A CHIN.

BUT THEN, AFTER YOU SPEND ABOUT THE FIRST FIVE MINUTES
WITH HIM YOU REALIZE, IT'S NOT JUST THE WAY HE LOOKS. IT'S
THE WAY HE IS.

LIKE, TO TAKE AN EXAMPLE, WHEN HE'S HAVING A FRESCA–HE
GETS HIMSELF A FRESCA FOR EXAMPLE, BUT HE DOESN'T OFFER
ANYONE ELSE ONE.

AND WHEN YOU ASK HIM, CAN YOU HAVE A FRESCA TOO, ALL HE
DOES IS, HE SHRUGS, AND HE SAYS, "IF YOU WANT ONE, YOU CAN
GET IT FOR YOURSELF." OF COURSE, HE DOESN'T LOOK AT YOU
WHEN HE'S SAYING THIS. BUT ALL OF A SUDDEN HE GETS UP AND
JUMPS UP TO TOUCH THE CEILING. FOR NO REASON YOU CAN
THINK OF.

ALL THAT FOR A FRESCA? YOU WONDER, AND THEN YOU THINK, WHAT WOULD THIS GUY BE LIKE IF HE WAS HAVING A SANDWICH?

AND THEN IT SO HAPPENS ONE DAY YOU'RE OUT AT A LITTLE RESTAURANT IN A MALL, WHERE YOU'D LEAST EXPECT IT. BUT THERE'S BILL G. AND HE'S <u>HAVING</u> A SANDWICH. THE THING IS, THOUGH, WHILE HE'S HAVING THE SANDWICH HE'S ALSO TALKING TOO LOUD FOR BEING IN A RESTAURANT. SO YOU FINALLY HAVE TO GO OVER AND ASK HIM TO KEEP IT DOWN, SO YOU AND THE OTHER DINERS CAN HAVE CONVERSATIONS OF YOUR OWN.

OF COURSE, HE STILL DOESN'T LOOK AT YOU WHEN YOU TALK TO HIM, BUT YOU CAN TELL HE DIDN'T EVEN <u>KNOW</u> HE WAS TALKING TOO LOUD.

AND THAT'S WHEN YOU REALIZE—BILL G. HAS JUST NEVER GROWN UP, AND HE DOESN'T EVEN KNOW IT. ALL THE THINGS HE DOES— WHETHER IT'S HAVING A FRESCA OR JUMPING UP TO TOUCH THE CEILING, OR TALKING TOO LOUD IN A RESTAURANT—ARE THE VERY SAME THINGS HE DID AS A CHILD.

AND THAT, MR. PRESIDENT, IS WHAT MAKES BILL G. SUCH A GEEK. HE'S A CHILD IN A GROWN-UP'S BODY, AND HE DOESN'T EVEN KNOW IT.

WELL, THOSE ARE MY PERSONAL OBSERVATIONS ON BILL G. I HOPE I DIDN'T GO ON AND ...

DALE, THAT WHOLE SPEECH WAS AWFULLY BORING. AND EVERYTHING YOU SAID WAS RANDOM TO THE MAX. AND THAT PART ABOUT, <u>BILL G.</u> IS <u>LIKE</u> A <u>CHILD</u>? THAT'S THE STUPIDEST THING I'VE EVER ... HOW AM I DOING?

135

MR. PRESIDENT, FOR A MOMENT THERE, YOU HAD GEEK WRITTEN ALL OVER YOU.

LET ME ASK YOU ONE QUESTION, THOUGH, DALE. DON'T WE ALL, DEEP-DOWN, WANT TO STAY A CHILD, EVEN WHEN WE'VE GOT A GROWN UP'S BODY?

YOU MEAN, DEEP-DOWN, WE <u>WANT</u> TO BE GEEKS?

OK, MAYBE BEING A GEEK ISN'T LOOKING SO BAD, AFTER ALL, IF IT MEANS I CAN DO WHATEVER I FEEL LIKE DOING. BECAUSE RIGHT NOW I FEEL LIKE TAKING BILL G. OUT TO THE WOODSHED, AND GIVING HIM A GOOD OLD ARKANSAS WHUPPING.

LET'S STOP OFF FOR A BURGER FIRST, SIR, AND SEE IF THE FEELING PASSES.

THE "GQ" BASIC QUESTION
#3

DO YOU...
WEAR "GEEKCHIC" THAT LOOKS ALIEN?

AUTHENTIC GOGGLE-STYLE GOGGLES →

← BOYISH HAIRSTYLE WORN SINCE BOYHOOD

WHO'S THE BOSS? GEEKS DON'T CARE

TOP BUTTON DONE THINKING OF MOM

← SPORTY ACCESSORY

BULGING BAG ADDS STYLISH OOMPH →

GEEK POWER (CORD)

BAGGY SEAT FOR ENDURANCE SITTING

SNEAKERS SEND MESSAGE, "I AM A PLAYER"

GQ #3.1 DO YOU ...
WEAR "GEEK-CHIC" THAT LOOKS ALIEN? +3
AND WAS NEVER IN A FASHION MAGAZINE? +4
DESPITE THE FACT THAT IT'S A CLASSIC? +2

THE MORE YOU KNOW, THE LESS YOU NEED.

GEEKCHIC IS A PRIMER FOR LIVING WELL BUT SENSIBLY.

QUALITY OF LIFE COMES NOT FROM ACCUMULATING THINGS

BUT IN PARING DOWN TO THE ESSENTIALS—

A SIMPLE PHILOSOPHY FOR COMPLICATED TIMES.

KNOW THE CODE.

CAN'T SEE WITHOUT THESE.
PERCEPTION IS IMPORTANT.

THE IDEA IS TO
BE NOTICED
FOR WHAT YOU
ACCOMPLISH.

WHILE THE DESK IS AN
INTEGRAL PART OF
THIS OUTFIT, THE
CHAIR PLAYS AN OFTEN
OVERLOOKED ROLE.

A MIX OF ELECTRONIC DEVICES WORKS
BECAUSE OF THE MONOCHROMATIC
COLOR SCHEME.

WHY DOES GEEKCHIC NEVER MAKE
THE COVERS OF FASHION MAGAZINES?

IT LOOKS GOOD ON ANYONE.

IT LOOKS AS RIGHT WITH JEANS AS IT DOES UNDER A "SMART"
SUIT JACKET.

ITS NEUTRAL "COLORS" AND "DURABLE" FABRICS GO WITH
ABSOLUTELY ANYTHING—AND STILL LOOK GOOD ON THEIR OWN.

INDEED, GEEKCHIC IS CLASSIC—BUT AS ANY GEEK WHO HAS STUDIED
CLASSICS KNOWS, CLASSICS ARE DULL , UNLIKE THE COVERS OF
FASHION MAGAZINES.

NEUTRAL
"COLORS"

LEVENG
#43
GEEK

"SMART"
SUIT JACKET

"DURABLE" FABRICS

YOU CAN TELL A LOT ABOUT A GEEK IN
THE FIRST SEVEN SECONDS AFTER MEETING, JUST FROM THE KIND
OF GEEKCHIC YOU NOTICE.

WISE GEEK IN
PROFESSORIAL
TWEED

FORWARD-THINKING
GEEK IN COLLEGIATE
CARDIGAN

DEAL-MAKING GEEK
IN POWER PLAID

STANDARD-BEARER
NERD, CONFUSING
PROFESSIONALISM
WITH WEARING A TIE

HIP, CREATIVE GEEK, WITH A GAP BETWEEN THE TEETH

GEEK GQ SCORE = 186
HALL OF DAVID
FAME LETTERMAN

FAMOUS GEEK QUOTES FROM DAVE:

"ONLY IN AMERICA COULD A GEEK LIKE ME ACHIEVE THE POSITION I HAVE."

"A GEEK IS A NERD IS A GAP-TOOTHED DORK, AND BY ANY OTHER NAME IS AS MUCH A TWIT. TO PARAPHRASE THAT CRAZY GERTRUDE STEIN."

A HEARTFELT LETTER FROM DAVE'S VIEWER E-MAIL BAG

I'M 29 NOW AND I'VE WATCHED AND ADMIRED DAVE SINCE I WAS 13, WHEN I SAW A FELLOW GEEK WHO SEEMED TO BE ENJOYING THE HELL OUT OF HIMSELF. THIS INTERNAL KODAK MOMENT, IF YOU WILL, MADE ME CONFIDENT THAT WHILE MY GEEKINESS WAS AN OBSTACLE IN THE LIFE OF AN ADOLESCENT GIRL, THERE WAS HOPE THAT MY TOTAL DWEEBNESS MIGHT ACTUALLY BE AN ENDEARING QUALITY AS AN ADULT.

NOT ONLY DO I LOVE DAVE FOR THIS REASON, I ALSO LOVE HIM BECAUSE HE'S TRULY A COMIC GENIUS.

141

EVOLUTION OF THE GEEK

THE QUESTION OF WHICH INDIVIDUALS WILL GENERALLY SURVIVE AND PROCREATE THEIR KIND DEPENDS ON THE SURVIVAL OF THE FITTEST. NATURALLY, THE QUESTION ARISES, WHY WASN'T THE GEEK WEEDED OUT BY EVOLUTION LONG AGO?

AND THE ANSWER HAS ONLY RECENTLY BEEN DISCOVERED.

GEEKCHIC = ENDURANCE

IN OTHER WORDS, GEEKS CAN WORK LONGER, AND GAIN AN ADVANTAGE THAT ENABLES THEM TO SURVIVE AND PROCREATE THEIR OWN KIND, AGAINST ALL ODDS, BECAUSE THEY HAVE CLOTHES THAT DON'T BIND.

IF YOU WANT TO SURVIVE, YOU MUST ASK YOURSELF: WHERE DO YOU "FIT" IN THE NEW GEEKCHIC PARADIGM?

AND TO ANSWER THAT YOU'VE GOT TO KNOW WHAT WORKS ... AND WHAT DOESN'T. THE WAY WILLIAM GATES III DOES.

GEEK HALL OF FAME

GQ SCORE = 225

WILLIAM H. GATES III

THE DETAILS

EARNED 10.9 US$ BILLION IN 1996—ABOUT 30 MILLION A DAY—FOR A TOTAL NET WORTH OF 23 BILLION, MAKING WILLIAM "BILL" GATES BY FAR THE WEALTHIEST INDIVIDUAL IN THE WORLD.

WHAT ARE THE GEEKCHIC TACTICS THAT ENABLE BILL TO SURVIVE?

LOW MAINTENANCE, WRINKLE-FREE, MACHINE WASHABLE FABRICS.

THE COLLAR MUST FIT CLOSELY AROUND THE NECK WITHOUT CUTTING OFF CIRCULATION.

SLEEVES SHOULD END AT WRIST, BUT FOREARM IS CLOSE ENOUGH.

WHETHER CALIFORNIA DENIM OR KEROUAC KHAKI, YOU'VE GOT TO UNDERSTAND THE RISE AND FALL OF PANTS.

GEEKCHIC FAQ—HOW LONG SHOULD PANTS BE?

ANSWER—LONGER THAN THEY ARE.

BEST SOLUTION: SO MUCH MONEY NO ONE CAN TELL IF YOU WEAR PANTS.

SEAMS SHOULD BE SECURELY SEWN DOWN.

143

ARE YOU AN FBI GEEK
INVESTIGATING THE PARANORMAL?

GEEK
HALL OF
FAME

GQ SCORE = 192

DANA KATHERINE
SCULLY, MD

THE DETAILS:

BIRTHDATE: FEBRUARY 23, 1964
HEIGHT: 5' 2
HAIR: AUBURN
EYES: BLUE
EDUCATION: B.S. PHYSICS,
UNIVERSITY OF MARYLAND, 1986
MEDICAL DEGREE (UNKNOWN),
RESIDENCY IN FORENSIC
PATHOLOGY.
PUBLICATIONS: SENIOR THESIS:
"EINSTEIN'S TWIN PARADOX: A NE
INTERPRETATION."
CURRENT RANK: SPECIAL AGENT
WEAPON: SMITH AND WESSON
1056 (9MM ROUNDS)

SCULLY'S TRAINING IN FORENSIC
MEDICINE AND PATHOLOGY
ALLOWS HER TO INVESTIGATE
THE OFTEN-BIZARRE EVIDENCE O
THE X-FILES WITH GEEKY
OBJECTIVITY.

PRAGMATIC, DOWN-TO-EARTH
DANA SCULLY IS SKEPTICAL OF
ANYTHING PARANORMAL,
BELIEVING THAT EVERYTHING
HAS A LOGICAL, SCIENTIFICALLY
GEEKIFIED EXPLANATION.

SCULLY HAS BEEN ABDUCTED BY
MYSTERIOUS FORCES AND
POSSIBLY SUBJECTED TO ALIEN
EXPERIMENTATION.

DANA SCULLY IS PORTRAYED BY
GILLIAN ANDERSON.

BUT WHAT IF WE DON'T WANT TO BE GEEKS?

THREE WORDS: GET OVER IT.

REMEMBER WHEN YOU GOT SENT HOME FOR WEARING INAPPROPRIATE CLOTHES ON DRESS-DOWN DAY?

WELL, WITH THE DRESS-DOWN FRIDAY BECOMING A WEEK-LONG PHENOMENON, YOU MIGHT NEVER WORK AGAIN. LIKE IT OR NOT, IN THE LAST FOUR YEARS, NEARLY EVERY MAJOR CORPORATION HAS IMPOSED A CORPORATE DRESS CODE OF GEEKCHIC.

NOW IT'S MORE IMPORTANT THAN EVER TO DRESS APPROPRIATELY.

GEEKCHIC DON'TS

SIGN ON BACK, "KICK ME"

BIG HAIR DOESN'T FIT IN CUBICLE

POWER TIE THAT CLIPS ON

NOT ERGONOMICALLY DESIGNED

POWER-FLY THAT WON'T STAY UP

HEMLINE CAUSES CONFUSION OVER MEANING OF "LAPTOP"

AT THE MORE PROGRESSIVE COMPANIES, SUCH AS BUREAUCRACIES, MONOPOLIES AND FORTUNE 10s, EMPLOYEES OFTEN HAVE DIFFICULTY ADJUSTING, DRESSING SOMETIMES TOO FORMALLY, AND OTHER TIMES TOO REVEALINGLY. STILL OTHERS IN DESPERATION HAVE TAKEN TO THE RITUAL OF BURNING THEIR OLD CLOTHES, AND HAVING THEMSELVES EMBALMED.

GEEKCHIC FAQ-WHAT DO I DO WITH MY OLD UNWEARABLE SUITS?
ANSWER: HOLD ONTO THEM UNTIL YOU GET A NEW CEO.

145

YOU DON'T HAVE TO BE UPTIGHT TO BE SUCCESSFUL.
GEEKCHIC IS NOT A CONTRADICTION IN TERMS.
HERE'S A SNAPPY GUIDE TO NAVIGATING LIFE IN THE '90S.

UNLIKE TRADITIONAL CLOTHES, WHERE ANYBODY COULD WEAR TWO MATCHING PIECES, GEEKCHIC GIVES YOU NO EASY WAY OUT. YOU'VE GOT TO CHOOSE:

OBLIVIOUS-TO-IT-ALL BERMUDA SHORTS.

GEEK HALL OF FAME: ALBERT GORE JR.

GQ SCORE = 166

OR STUDIED CASUAL.

UNITED STATES VICE PRESIDENT
POPULARIZED TERM "INFORMATION SUPERHIGHWAY"
NICKNAMES: ALGOR THE ALIEN, ALGORHYTHM
BEST KNOW FOR: BEING STIFF. HAS TURNED THIS "ABILITY" TO REMARKABLE ADVANTAGE.
NOW CONSIDERED A LEADER AND INNOVATOR IN GEEKCHIC FOR THE "FLEXIBILITY CHALLENGED."

BRINGS OFF CASUAL LOOK, EVEN IN SUIT. ⟶
GRADUATE OF "STOP THE STIFFNESS" SEMINAR

WEARS WRINKLED JACKET, TO GIVE IMPRESSION OF BENDABLE JOINTS. ⟶

DEVIL-MAY-CARE LINT ON PANTS.

BECAUSE IN TODAY'S WORLD IT CAN BE DEADLY TO
LOOK AS IF YOU'RE TAKING CUES FROM A TWENTY-YEAR-OLD
DRESS-FOR-SUCCESS MANUAL, WHICH IS SO FIVE MINUTES AGO.

HOW TO SURVIVE AND EVEN FLOURISH WITH GEEKCHIC:
THREE STEPS OF WARDROBE REENGINEERING

1. THINK BASICS, VERSATILE ENOUGH TO PLAY A VARIETY OF
WARDROBE ROLES

2. USE COLOR AND PATTERN TO SUIT YOUR NEEDS

3. CHOOSE THE RIGHT LOW-KEY ACCESSORIES

1. BASIC VERSATILE
SHIRT-LIKE THING.
ALSO DOUBLES AS
HAND TOWEL

3. LOW-KEY ACCESSORIES:
NEW IMPROVED
POCKET-PROTECTOR
WITH SHARP EDGE

CLEVER DEVICES
ENCOURAGE OTHERS TO
COMMUNICATE FROM A
DISTANCE

2. THERE IS COLOR
BESIDES GRAY AND
NAVY BLUE.

THERE'S DIRTY
BROWN, FOR
INSTANCE.

AND JERRY GARCIA
TIE-DYE

DRESS UP WITH-
OUT PUTTING ON
A TIE OR HEELS.
CREATIVE USE OF
PATTERNS CAN
MAKE YOU LOOK AS
NATTY AS A
MONTY PYTHON
TWIT.

TO KNOW HOW TO ANSWER THAT
AGE-OLD QUESTION, WHAT AM I GOING TO WEAR TODAY?

YOU'VE GOT TO CHECK OUT YOUR CALENDAR BEFORE YOU CHECK OUT YOUR CLOSET.

IS THERE ROOM FOR THOSE SENTIMENTAL PIECES YOU BOUGHT FOR $1,800 IN A FIT OF TRENDINESS LAST AUGUST?

ANSWER: ONLY IF YOU'RE GOING TO THE MTV MUSIC AWARDS

GEEK   GQ SCORE = 151
HALL OF FAME   LISA KENNEDY MONTGOMERY

AN MTV VJ BEST KNOWN FOR PUBLICLY DECLARING BOTH HER CHASTITY AND HER GEEKINESS, AND AS THE PIONEER OF GEEKCHIC. HER GLASSES ARE HER ON-AIR SIGNATURE. SHE HAS 24 PAIRS AND REFUSES TO WEAR CONTACT LENSES EVEN WHEN OFFERED COMMERCIAL ENDORSEMENTS BY THE LENS COMPANIES—IN AN AGE WHEN CONTACT LENSES PROVIDE A READY DISGUISE FOR GEEKS IN DENIAL.

KENNEDY'S VERBAL AGILITY AND EXTEMPORIZED MONOLOGUES ARE FURTHER EVIDENCE OF HER GEEKINESS. IN THE SITCOM "MURPHY BROWN," THE GEEKY CHARACTER OF "MCGOVERN" WAS MODELED AFTER KENNEDY.

SOURCE: WWW.ALTCULTURE.COM

SOMETIMES YOU MIGHT WANT TO

SHOW YOUR ELAN WITH A WITTY MIX OF CLOTHES THAT SEND A SUBTEXT MESSAGE ABOUT YOUR PAST LIFE AS SUPERFICIAL POWER-BROKER.

THREE WORDS: GET OVER IT.

AND ON THOSE MORNINGS WHEN YOUR FLIGHT FROM HONG KONG WAS 6 HOURS LATE GETTING IN THE NIGHT BEFORE, AND NOW YOU'VE HAD 3 HOURS SLEEP BEFORE A 7:30 AM PRESENTATION, AND YOUR BODY IS SAYING, "TAKE ME I'M YOURS" – YOU MIGHT WANT TO REACH FOR THE REASSURING PINSTRIPE ON THE PLASTIC HANGER.

THREE WORDS: DON'T DO IT.

RELY ON GEEKCHIC TO SIMPLIFY YOUR LIFE. GEEKCHIC IS MEANT FOR JUST THOSE TIMES WHEN YOU'RE WORKING HARDER THAN YOU'VE EVER WORKED BEFORE.

REMEMBER THE SIMPLE GEEKCHIC MOTTO –

THREE WORDS:
DRESS FOR DURESS

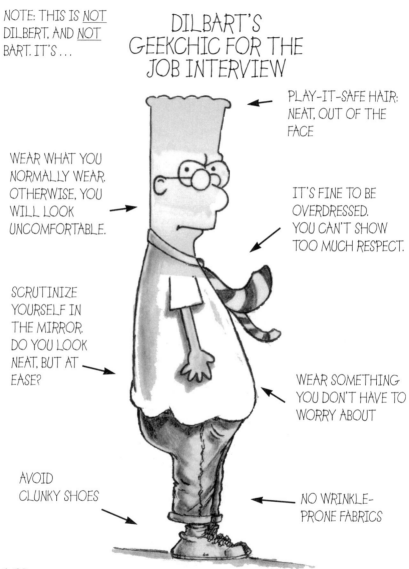

THE "GQ" BASIC QUESTION
2
DO YOU... USE "GEEKSPEAK"
THAT SOUNDS ALIEN?

NYETSCAPE

I'M AWKWARD, YOU'RE AWKWARD, AND THAT'S OK   153

GQ #2.1 DO YOU ...
USE "GEEKSPEAK" THAT SOUNDS ALIEN? +3
WHICH YOU CALL "JUST NECESSARY"? +2
BECAUSE "REAL GEEKS DON'T EAT CLICHÉ"? +4

THE WAY THAT GEEKS TALK—ALWAYS USING TRICKY
DOUBLE-MEANINGS BUT NEVER ANY FACIAL EXPRESSION—IS
CALLED "GEEKSPEAK."

WHETHER TECHNICAL JARGON, PSYCHO-BABBLE, OR PLAIN OLD
IG-PAY ATIN-LAY, GEEKSPEAK, TO A NON-GEEK, SOUNDS TOTALLY
ALIEN, AND THAT'S NOT GIVING ALIENS ANY CREDIT. BUT TO
GEEKS, GEEKSPEAK IS "JUST NECESSARY." IT'S THE ONLY WAY
GEEKS HAVE OF COPING WITH A LIFE THAT'S COMPLICATED—
AND THAT CAN'T BE DESCRIBED BY THE USUAL CLICHÉS.

BECAUSE REAL GEEKS DON'T EAT CLICHÉ. STALE,
WARMED OVER, LEFTOVER, OR REGURGITATED—HOWEVER THE
CLICHÉ MIGHT BE SERVED, GEEKS WILL ALWAYS SEND IT BACK,
UN-TOUCHEÉD.

It's been one of those **SALMON DAYS,** where you feel like you've been running upstream for all you're worth, only to wind up in a **GAS-FIRED GRILL** belonging to the competition.

like Shakespeare's happy salad days, without the happy salad

also called, getting smoked

What you figure you need is just a little **client-server action.**

connection, the possibility of intercourse

After all, you're **plug-and-play, A REAL NORMAL GEEK.** And since the internet **got RAM,**

not difficult at all, easy

figure of speech, like "a real wild nun"

became surprisingly interesting, after only slight improvement

you've been *having an Elvis year!*

the most popular you've ever been

154

Your only problem is, you've been *under mouse arrest* for too long.

a feeling of being handcuffed to the mouse

So you decide to
juice your brick.

rejuvenate your drained ego; also, charge a battery, especially a very large one

First, you do a little
EGO-SURFING—

searching the internet for your own name

slurp your guestbook

read comments of visitors to your home page

ROBOT YOUR LINK-TO'S,
—that kind of thing.

search the internet for links to your home page

Then, feeling **certifiably** GEEKY, you **take your 3D avatar** out the door.

as opposed to doubtfully, or questionably geeky

the real world representation of you

Still you feel empty
in a physical way. — due to the laws of physics

So you stop off for a quick
Dorito syndrome . — desire for snack food

At the register, though, you **LURK...** — watch closely

and indeed, you detect — shop-lifting in reverse

scanner-lifting. — having a computer malfunction

"Hey," you tell the clerk,
"You're going down."

"These are $1.99 on special"

Outside again, you
launch your underpowered browser — take your knockabout car

on the
asphalt highway. — on the road

156

You search around a little but
the **first hit you get** — first place you try
turns out to be a **COBWEB SITE**. — uninteresting, not hip

Too much **adminisphere**— an atmosphere clouded by administration
you need a **HASSLEWORD** — hassled by a password
at the door.

Of course,

"ALPHA GEEK"
is all you have to say,
and you go right in.

— the most knowledgeable geek in a group of geeks; variations are— biggest geek, geekiest geek, über geek

But inside, they're all *tourists*, — visitors to geekdom
and **open-collar workers,** — those who work at home
pretending to be
warriors of DOOM. — expert in the most popular computer game in history

Well, you figure,
if you're about to **CRASH,**
you might as well have a
MID-AIR PASSENGER EXCHANGE.

the ultimate fate of all computer users, as in, "Help, I've crashed, and I can't get up"

a term pilots and air-traffic controllers use for a near-miss

So you approach the first
GODDESS
at your altitude.

But GOING IN TO TAKE A CLOSER LOOK,
you seem to observe a
bad case of *keyboard plaque.*

worn from over-use, covered with a layer of detritus

Well, you're not a **nerd-basher**
and so you say to her,

"Do you want to
   squirt the bird?"

communicate with the rocket ship

She gives you a look like
she's still GLAZING OVER
from some very early morning meeting.

derivative of MEGO, "my eyes glaze over"

And all she says is,
"Nyetscape."

not Netscape, or more broadly, just "not"

What kind of **crapplet** is that, you ask yourself. This GODDESS looks like she **works in a vomit comet,** and she's giving YOU **the shut down**?

a kind of internet program, especially one poorly written

the NASA test area for motion sickness

"WELL, IT'S A FEATURE," you tell her. Just so she won't *think you're a dork.*

the Geek's response to any error, meaning "I meant to do that"

a variation of a Geek, somehow even less fashionable

But secretly, you're wondering if you might have **link rot.**

a connection that no longer works

You decide to **have a beepilepsy,** and TAKE YOUR PACKETS RIGHT THE HELL HOME.

a sudden change in mental state typical of someone whose beeper has just gone off

what you do when you don't want to play on the internet anymore

159

On your way out, you find yourself
in graybar land.
Joining the world-wide wait.

a bar, usually gray, that appears on a computer screen during a computer delay

20 million users of the World-Wide Web, all waiting together for...

When, suddenly—the **SERVER COMES UP**
and you **make a bookmark**——

a response from the server

note, in order to remember

GODDESS with
OBJECT VALUE——

more than superficial appeal

pointing her browser
right at you.

navigating purposefully

It's **A CRITICAL MOMENT**——

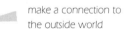

an important test

naturally, your SYNAPSES FAIL—
all you get is **brain fart.**

a neurological malfunction— and its result

Before you can even
GET THE PIPE TO GO LIVE,
you realize you **have a mirror.**

make a connection to the outside world

an exact duplicate

And he's **already
downloading** .

communicating, sending information

"Do you want to **squirt the bird**?"
he says to this GODDESS,
copying your whole disk.

stealing your lines

an internet programmer,
stiff as the plastic action figure

Obviously, he's a real **CGI Joe,**
right in **your gateway.**

your connection to
the outside world

YOUR SCREEN GOES BLANK.

Next to him, you feel like a
dead tree edition.

the unnecessary,
paper version of
an online
newspaper

You might as well just
START A BEGATHON,

an appeal to
ones' good
nature, as in
charitable
fund-raising

BUT right then,
the network gods smile
upon you.

the unexpected
resolution of a
problem

YOUR GODDESS
gives Joe a 404
—it's like he's not even there.

an internet error
message, meaning
no connection

And WITHOUT ANY DESCRAMBLING,
she **pops into YOUR monitor**,
and you HAVE AUDIO.

"DEBUG HIM,"

she says to you, nodding at Joe,
"HE'S **chip jewelry**."

straightforwardly, wihout disguise

show the error of, give the lie to

obsolete microchip whose only use is decorative

Quickly, **YOU MESSAGE** Joe.
"GEEK BUDDY,"
You say, "POSSIBLE CAREER LIMITING MOVE."

send a message, in this case, to Joe

a choice resulting in an undesired effect

Because GEEKS prefer GROUPWARE,
even when their LINES CROSS—
you just never know when
you might *NEED A CONSULT*.

benefit gained only in a group

telephone lines incorrectly switched

advice given as a professional courtesy

Then she gives you
MORE BANDWIDTH
"You, on the other hand ..."
your GODDESS says, "WHATTAGEEK."
Her voice crackles in your sPEAKeRS.

greater capacity for exchange

meant perversely, as high praise

Your eyes get big—
your mouth drops open.

You **print a smiley** of surprise. **8-o**

arrange characters to depict facial expression

Reentry, and SPLASHDOWN—
Houston, do you read.

an announcement by
ground control that the
capsule has landed

"AND YOU," you finally find the words,
searching a vast index in her eyes,
"BLOW MY BUFFER."

momentarily lose
one's senses

Of course, you know this
little START ME UP
is your emotional *spike*.
And any **CLOCK CYCLE** now
you'll be **batmobiling** like crazy,
sensitivity fenders up, reading from
your instruments.

the on position of
the on/off switch

peak in a wave form

the smallest measurable
unit of time

surround with a
protective shell

GQ #2.2 DO YOU ...
HAVE A LOVE-HATE RELATIONSHIP?
WITH "LOVE"?
WHERE THE ONLY PART YOU HATE IS
"THE RELATIONSHIP"?

+1

+4

+3

Trying to make sure nobody gets
COMMENTED OUT,
in any sort of an irrational,
impossibly complex
relationship.

to take out, after
putting in

ELECTRONIC JOURNAL OF BILL G/

12/31/99 11:48 PM PST
GEEKSPEAK TOP 10 PERSONAL FAVORITES

#10 GEEKERATI: SAME AS LITERATI (PEOPLE WHO LIKE BOOKS) AND
GLITTERATI (PEOPLE WHO LIKE MOVIES). BUT GEEKERATI ARE
PEOPLE WHO LIKE ME.

#9 COMPUTER IS "POWER": SO IS NUCLEAR ENERGY. NOBODY WANTS
THAT IN HOME, EITHER.

#8 CONTENT IS "KING": REALLY MORE OF A PRINCE, WAITING FOR
ME TO STEP DOWN.

#7 NEW: DOESN'T WORK YET.

#6 REVOLUTIONARY: BET YOU CAN'T TELL IT'S STILL THE SAME.

#5 FRICTION-FREE INTERACTIVITY: INTERPERSONAL RELATIONSHIP
WITHOUT GETTING PERSONAL. BIG IMPROVEMENT IN BUSINESS. NOT
MUCH DIFFERENCE IN PERSONAL LIFE.

#4 VIRTUAL REALITY: MEANS NEVER HAVING TO SAY YOU'RE SORRY.

#3 WORLD-WIDE WEB: NEW WAY OF COMMUNICATING. MAYBE BETTER
LUCK THIS TIME.

#2 FIRE, AIM, HEY, WHY WEREN'T YOU READY: WHAT CEOS DO FOR
A LIVING

#1 I.P. ADDRESS: METHOD FOR STAKING OUT TERRITORY ON
INTERNET. WORKS FOR DOGS. WHY NOT CYBERSPACE.

THE "GQ" BASIC QUESTION
#1
DO YOU...EVER GET ENOUGH "SEX"?

GQ #1.1 DO YOU ...
EVER GET ENOUGH
"SEX"?

+3

HOW MANY TIMES HAVE YOU HEARD SOMEONE SAY, "HE'S A GEEK, HE'S NICE, HE'S SMART ... WHY DOESN'T HE HAVE SOMEONE SPECIAL IN HIS LIFE?"

FRANKLY, MANY GEEKS FIND IT EASIER TO LAUNCH A PUBLIC OFFERING, SWITCH MUSICAL INSTRUMENTS IN MID-PERFORMANCE, OR TRAVEL AROUND THE WORLD IN A HOT AIR BALLOON THAN TO FIND THAT SPECIAL PERSON.

THE ONLY WORKABLE SOLUTION IS FOR THAT SPECIAL PERSON TO TAKE MATTERS INTO HER OWN HANDS.

WOMEN WHO LOVE GEEKS TOO MUCH—THE RULES, IS A COLLECTION OF THE SIMPLE DO'S AND DON'TS FOR FINDING MR. GEEK, WHEN HE CAN'T POSSIBLY FIND YOU.

you goddess, you

RULE #1

BE A
UNIQUE
AND
SPECIAL CREATURE

BE YOURSELF. YOU ARE ...

GODDESS TO ALL GEEKS
IN THE GALAXY.

JUST BEING A CREATURE
WON'T HELP,
UNLESS YOUR
MR. GEEK IS
IN BIOLOGY.

DON'T'S

DO'S

meeting mr. geek

RULE #2

DON'T TALK TO HIM FIRST

IF YOU WAITED FOR MR. GEEK TO TALK TO YOU FIRST, YOUR BIOLOGICAL CLOCK WOULD SURELY RUN OUT. AND SLAM THE DOOR SCREAMING.

DO'S

DON'T'S

ALL INITIATIVE MUST COME FROM YOU. BUT SIMPLY TALKING TO MR. GEEK MAY NOT BE ENOUGH. BECAUSE IT IS QUITE LIKELY THAT MR. GEEK MAY NOT BE LISTENING—SEE RULE 3.

meeting mr. geek

RULE #3

DON'T
TALK TO
HIM
IF HE'S
A GEEK

HOW TO TELL IF MR. GEEK IS LISTENING.

ASK HIM ANY QUESTION, LIKE, "AM I TALKING TOO MUCH?" OR, "AM I WEARING UNDERWEAR?" IF MR. GEEK ANSWERS SOMETHING LIKE, "OH! GOOD POINT!" AND SOUNDS SUSPICIOUSLY POLITE—SEE RULE 4.

DO'S

DON'T'S

meeting mr. geek

RULE #4

DON'T TALK— WHY BOTHER.

MR. GEEK ALWAYS PAYS ATTENTION WHEN HE IS READING. NOT ONLY THAT, HE ACTUALLY REMEMBERS WHAT HE IS READING.

SO GIVE MR. GEEK SOMETHING HE'LL REMEMBER, SEND HIM E-MAIL. WRITE HIM A NOTE. SAVE YOUR BREATH.

DON'TS

DO'S

meeting mr. geek

RULE #4A

THERE'S
NOTHING
MORE
TO
SAY

IT WORKS LIKE THIS:
HE LOVES TO READ. YOU
GIVE HIM THINGS TO READ.
HE LOVES YOU. IT'S LIKE
TRAINING A PUPPY.

DO'S

AFTER A COUPLE
OF GOOD OLD-
FASHIONED
NOTES, OR "LOVE
E-LETTERS," BUT
WELL BEFORE
YOUR
BIOLOGICAL
CLOCK CAN COUNT TO 40,
MR. GEEK WILL BECOME
YOUR MR. GEEK. AND YOU
WILL BE HIS GODDESS.

DON'T'S

meeting mr. geek
RULE #4B

DON'T
TALK
TOO MUCH
OR DID I
ALREADY SAY
THAT.

YOU CAN NEVER GIVE MR. GEEK TOO MUCH TO READ, OR TALK TOO MUCH.

BECAUSE IF HE'S NOT TALKING WITH YOU, OR READING SOMETHING YOU GAVE HIM, HE COULD BE TALKING OR READING WITH SOMEONE ELSE—MAYBE A ROMANTIC RUSSIAN, WRITING 1200 PAGE E-MAILS OVER THE INTERNET. OR WORSE YET, AN ENGLISH LIT MAJOR, WHO CAN TYPE REALLY FAST.

DON'T'S

DO'S

meeting mr. geek

RULE #5

DON'T
ASK
HIM
TO DANCE

AS FOR DANCING, DON'T
EXPECT MUCH. HE'LL
FOLLOW YOU, IF YOU START.
BUT IT WON'T BE PRETTY.

DON'T'S

DO'S

meeting mr. geek

RULE #6

DON'T
STARE
AT
MEN

NOT STARING AT MR. GEEK ISN'T MUCH OF A PROBLEM. OH SURE, YOU THINK HE'S "CUTE." THE WAY HE FOLLOWS YOU AROUND WHEN HE'S WITH YOU.

BUT A LOT OF THE TIME, HE'S NOT REALLY WITH YOU—HE'S IN CYBERSPACE, OR JUST PLAIN SPACE.

DON'T'S

DO'S

calling mr. geek

RULE #7

DON'T
CALL
HIM

NOT CALLING MR. GEEK WOULD
ONLY CONFUSE HIM, FURTHER.

IF YOU DON'T CALL, YOUR MR.
GEEK FORGETS EVERYTHING
YOU TOLD HIM. LAUNDRY,
GROCERIES, BANK. ALL OF
IT, OUT THE DRAFTY
OPEN WINDOW OF HIS
GEEK MIND.

DO'S

CALLING
HIM, ABOUT ONCE AN HOUR,
SIMPLY REMINDS HIM TO
FOLLOW HIS GODDESS, EVEN
WHEN SHE IS NOT WITH HIM.

DON'T'S

calling mr. geek

RULE #8

RARELY
RETURN
HIS
CALLS

AS A GODDESS, YOU ALWAYS RETURN EVERYBODY'S PHONE CALLS—AND MR. GEEK CERTAINLY RETURNS YOURS. YOU'RE HIS GODDESS. AND IT'S THE GEEK WAY.

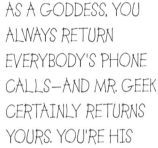

DO'S

DON'T'S

THE COMPLETE GEEK (AN OPERATING MANUAL)

dating mr. geek

RULE #9

DON'T
ACCEPT
A SATURDAY
NIGHT DATE
AFTER
WEDNESDAY

DON'T ACCEPT THE CONCEPT OF "A SATURDAY NIGHT DATE." IT IS TOO CLOSELY RELATED TO THE CONCEPT OF BEING "WITHOUT A DATE ON SATURDAY NIGHT."

AND YOU WOULDN'T BE, EXCEPT THAT YOUR MR. GEEK IS PROBABLY OFF SOMEWHERE WORKING.

DO'S

WHICH IS WHY ON SATURDAY NIGHT GODDESSES EVERYWHERE USUALLY MAKE A DATE WITH A BOOK.

DON'T'S

dating mr. geek
RULE #10

DON'T
MEET HIM
HALFWAY
OR GO
DUTCH
ON A DATE

MEETING "HALFWAY" IS VERY GEEKY. IT'S ONE OF THE HIGHER PRINCIPLES, RIGHT UP THERE WITH "DO YOU WANT HALF?"

AS FOR WHO PAYS, GODDESSES DON'T MAKE A BIG DEAL ABOUT IT. FACE IT, YOU'VE BOTH GOT MONEY.

DO'S

DON'T'S

ONE MORE THING, GODDESSES DON'T CALL IT A "DUTCH DATE" UNLESS THEIR MR. GEEK IS DUTCH.

dating mr. geek

RULE #11

FILL UP YOUR
TIME BEFORE
THE DATE

YOUR TIME IS ALREADY
FILLED, THANK YOU. THIS IS
THE REASON YOU HAVE A
DATEBOOK.

DO'S

DON'T'S

RULE #12

ALWAYS END THE DATE
FIRST

ALWAYS END THE DAY, FIRST.
IF THAT MEANS MR. GEEK
COMES IN SECOND, OH WELL.

dating mr. geek

RULE #13

STOP
DATING HIM
IF HE DOESN'T
BUY YOU
ROMANTIC GIFTS

STOP DATING HIM IF ALL YOU'RE WORRIED ABOUT IS WHAT HE BUYS YOU. DON'T BE "DATED."

STOP AND LOOK AT YOURSELF. YOU ARE A MAGNIFICENT GODDESS. THAT IS YOUR GIFT.

DO'S

DON'T'S RULE #14

BE SMART ABOUT YOUR DATES

BE SMART. AND MAKE SURE YOUR DATES ARE.

181

sex with mr. geek

RULE #15

NO MORE
THAN CASUAL KISSING
ON THE FIRST DATE

NO MORE THAN CASUAL SEX ON THE FIRST DATE. MR. GEEK WILL WANT TO BE FORMAL ABOUT IT, BUT IT'S NOT AS MUCH FUN.

DO'S

DON'T'S

RULE #16

DON'T RUSH INTO SEX

DON'T RUSH DURING SEX. MR. GEEK LIKES TO TAKE HIS TIME WITH EVERYTHING. SOMETIMES THIS HAS ITS ADVANTAGES.

sex with mr. geek

RULE #17

LET HIM
TAKE
THE
LEAD

LET HIM PUT THE LEAD IN HIS PENCIL. MR. GEEK IS SURPRISINGLY GOOD AT THIS.

DON'T'S RULE #18 DO'S

DON'T SEE HIM MORE THAN ONCE OR TWICE A WEEK

DON'T HAVE SEX WITH HIM MORE THAN ONCE OR TWICE AN HOUR. IF MR. GEEK DIES, YOU'LL MISS HIM.

relating to mr. geek

RULE #19

DON'T
TELL HIM WHAT TO
DO

DON'T TELL MR. GEEK WHAT
TO DO, MORE THAN ONCE.
THE SECOND TIME, SEND HIM
E-MAIL. HE PROBABLY WASN'T
PAYING
ATTENTION.

DON'T'S

DO'S

RULE #20

BE HONEST
BUT MYSTERIOUS

BE HONEST WHEN YOU'RE
MYSTIFIED. SOMETIMES
MR. GEEK WILL DO
THINGS THAT LEAVE YOU
SAYING, HUH?

relating to mr. geek

RULE #21

DON'T
LIVE
WITH
A MAN

DON'T EXPECT TO LIVE WITH MR. GEEK. HE PROBABLY DOESN'T HAVE A LIFE. HE AND ALL HIS THINGS MIGHT "LIVE" IN THE SMALLEST POSSIBLE CLOSET. REMEMBER. HE ONLY REALLY NEEDS TO "LIVE" WHEN HE IS SLEEPING. AND THIS YOU WILL RARELY SEE HIM DO.

DO'S

DON'T'S

RULE #22

BE EASY
TO LIVE
WITH

BE EASY TO LIVE WITHOUT. BECAUSE MR. GEEK MAY OFTEN HAVE TO BE AWAY AT WORK—AND LIVING WITHOUT YOU IS HARD FOR HIM TO DO.

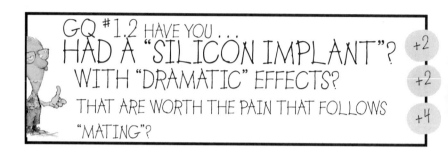

GQ #1.2 HAVE YOU ...
HAD A "SILICON IMPLANT"? +2
WITH "DRAMATIC" EFFECTS? +2
THAT ARE WORTH THE PAIN THAT FOLLOWS
"MATING"? +4

FORTUNATELY FOR GEEKS, SCIENCE IS CONTINUING TO MAKE
DRAMATIC STRIDES IN THE SEARCH FOR A CURE FOR TOTAL
GEEKINESS. RECENTLY, SOME EXCITING DISCOVERIES HAVE
TAKEN PLACE, WHICH DEMONSTRATE THAT GEEKS REALLY
CAN HAVE A LIFE.

IN FACT IT APPEARS THAT THESE DISCOVERIES HAVE BEEN SO
EXCITING THAT A KIND OF BANDWAGON EFFECT HAS
OCCURRED, WITH PEOPLE WHO ARE NOT GEEKS
ATTEMPTING TO JUMP ON. GO FIGURE.

THE ONLY THING THAT MATTERS TO GEEKS IS THAT THERE
IS NOW HOPE. IN THE NEXT SECTION THE MOST DRAMATIC
RECENT DISCOVERY OF ALL IS DESCRIBED, FOR ANY GEEKS
WHO MIGHT NOT HAVE HEARD ABOUT IT YET, HAVING
SPENT THE LAST YEAR OR TWO IN TOTAL OBLIVION.

THE SILICON IMPLANT

NEWS FLASH: SCIENTISTS HAVE DISCOVERED THAT IMPLANTS OF SILICON (SYMBOL $$) IN A MAN HAVE THE SAME DRAMATIC BUT UNEXPLAINED EFFECT AS IMPLANTS OF SILICONE (SYMBOL >>) IN A WOMAN—MUCH BETTER PROSPECTS FOR MATING.

THE RESULTS ARE STILL EXPERIMENTAL, BUT A REPORT PUBLISHED IN THE NEW ENGLAND JOURNAL OF MEDICAL IMPLANTS CONCLUDES, "SILICON $$ IMPLANTED IN A MAN CERTAINLY INCREASES HIS CHANCES OF HAVING SEX, AT LEAST."

FDA APPROVAL FOR THE IMPLANT WILL NOT BE REQUIRED.

SILICON $$, UNLIKE SILICONE >>, CAN BE IMPLANTED NON-SURGICALLY. THE IMPLANT REQUIRES ONLY A DAILY EXPOSURE TO ANY SILICON $$ DEVICE, WHICH CAN BE CONVENIENTLY ADMINISTERED AT THE WORKPLACE.

SURPRISINGLY, THE "SILICON $$ IMPLANT" PROVED MOST EFFECTIVE IN MEN WHO INITIALLY HAD ZERO CHANCE OF HAVING SEX—A GROUP IDENTIFIED IN THE STUDY AS "GEEKS" (SYMBOL $\partial\Sigma$).

AFTER SILICON $$ IMPLANTING, THESE MEN, OR "GEEKS $\partial\Sigma$," HAD AMONG THE HIGHEST CHANCES OF HAVING SEX, EQUAL TO THE GROUP IDENTIFIED AS "STUDS" (SYMBOL !!).

STUDS !!, HOWEVER, DID NOT RECEIVE ANY SILICON $$. THEY MERELY CONTINUED THEIR USUAL DAILY EXPOSURE TO SILICONE >>.

—SIDE EFFECTS—

95% OF IMPLANTEES REPORTED THAT, WHILE QUITE PAINFUL, THE DAILY EXPOSURE TO SILICON WAS WORTH THE BENEFITS OF MATING.

THE OTHER 5% FOUND THE EXPOSURE TO BE RELATIVELY PAINLESS, COMPARED TO THE PAIN THEY EXPERIENCED FOLLOWING MATING.

OTHER REPORTED SIDE EFFECTS ARE NOT CONSIDERED SERIOUS. THESE INCLUDE ONSET OF PERSONALITY DISORDERS, OR "GEEKINESS," AND OCCASIONAL DIFFICULTY PASSING THROUGH METAL DETECTORS.

—THE EXPLANATION—

AT THIS TIME SCIENTISTS STILL HAVE NONE.

ALTHOUGH ONE THEORY SUGGESTS IT MAY BE A RESULT OF "PRECIPITOUS RISE IN INCOME."

THESE FIGURES ILLUSTRATE THE THEORY:

BEFORE IMPLANT:

AFTER IMPLANT:

SCRAWNY,
UNATTRACTIVE,
LOW-MATING CHANCES

SCRAWNY,
UNATTRACTIVE,
HIGH-MATING CHANCES

189

IN THE STUDY, THE WOMEN WHO CHOSE TO MATE WITH
THESE SILICON-IMPLANTED MEN WERE ASKED QUITE A FEW
QUESTIONS.

SUCH AS : WHY DID YOU MATE WITH HIM—WAS IT THE
IMPLANT?

(ACTUALLY, THIS ONE QUESTION WAS ASKED QUITE A FEW
TIMES, BY THE SCIENTISTS WHO COULD NOT BELIEVE WHAT
THEY HEARD.)

TYPICAL RESPONSES ARE LISTED BELOW:

THE SMALLER THE BETTER, THE LESSER THE SWEATING	2%
I NEVER EVEN NOTICED HE HAD ONE—IT LOOKS PERFECTLY NATURAL	8%
I DIDN'T MATE WITH HIM FOR HIS LOOKS	9%
I MATED WITH HIM FOR HIS PERSONALITY	81%

THE SCIENTISTS DID NOT REGARD THESE ANSWERS AS VALID,
HOWEVER, SINCE 98% OF THE WOMEN WERE CLEARLY LYING.

THIS SILICON $$ EFFECT AMONG MEN IS SO DRAMATIC, AND
YET UNEXPLAINABLE, AND EVEN SILLY, THAT SCIENTISTS HAVE
NOW TAKEN TO CALLING IT THE "SILLY ICON $$" EFFECT.

THE SILICONE >> EFFECT AMONG WOMEN IS ALSO CALLED THE
"SILLY CONE >>" EFFECT.

ALTHOUGH THE SILICON IMPLANT HAS ONLY RECENTLY BEEN
DISCOVERED, POPULAR REFERENCES TO IT ARE ALREADY NOW
HEARD ON THE STREET.

EXAMPLE

ELECTRONIC JOURNAL OF BILL G/

12/31/99 11:52 PM PST

JUST RECEIVED WARNING MESSAGE. HAVE LOST
CONTACT WITH PROJECT ZEKE. LAST SEEN ENTERING
INTERNET HOSTILE TERRITORY, SILICON VALLEY,
WHERE ANONYMOUS COMPETITORS ARE ALL HIDING.

ZEKE MAY HAVE HIT BAD STRETCH OF HIGHWAY. IF
PROJECT ZEKE DOES NOT REPORT BACK IN THE NEXT
60 SECONDS, WILL BE CONSIDERED MISSING. AND
POSSIBLY TERMINATED.

ONLY MINUTES BEFORE NEW MILLENNIUM EVE. PLANS
TO HAVE SCRAP-ZEKE PARTY MAY BE SCRAPPED.
NEXT THOUSAND YEARS REALLY STARTING OFF ON
WRONG FOOT. MAKE A NOTE: USE OMNIPOTENCE TO
RESET GREENWICH MEAN TIME, GET ONE MORE CRACK?

58 SECONDS, 57 SECONDS, 56 SECONDS, 55 SECONDS

EVERYTHING I NEEDED TO KNOW, I LEARNED LATE LAST NIGHT

GQ #1.3 HAVE YOU . . .
EVER CONNECTED SO "COMPLETELY"? +3
YOU LOST TRACK OF "THE MOMENT"? +3
AND THEN FOUND YOURSELF "69'D"? +5

SO I THOUGHT I'D STOP IN FOR A FEW MICROSECONDS AT A NEW MILLENNIUM EVE PARTY—WHILE BILL G. WAS BUSY SOMEWHERE, I DON'T KNOW, PLAYING GOLF WITH THE PRESIDENT OR SOMETHING—AND AS SOON AS I WENT THROUGH THE GATEWAY I SAW HER. MY GEEK GODDESS, WHO HAD HELPED ME THROUGH THE FIREWALL, AND WHO I THOUGHT I WOULD NEVER SEE AGAIN. SHE WAS OVER NEAR THE THOMAS HARDY SERVER BROWSING TESS OF THE D'URBERVILLES.

THIS TIME, I ASKED HER FOR HER NAME. "BILLIE," SHE TOLD ME. BILLIE GEEKS—OR BILLIE G. AS SHE PREFERRED TO BE CALLED. IT WAS A BEAUTIFUL NAME, AND IT HAD A FAMILIAR RING TO IT, AS IF WE HAD KNOWN EACH OTHER IN ANOTHER VIRTUAL REALITY.

RIGHT AWAY, THE TWO OF US CONNECTED—SO COMPLETELY IT WAS LIKE WE WERE THE ONLY TWO GEEKS ON THE INTERNET.

WE EVEN RODE THE FIREWALL A FEW TIMES TOGETHER, JUST FOR OLD TIMES SAKE. AND WE CHATTED. ACTUALLY, SHE CHATTED MOSTLY, BUT I LISTENED. AND I REALIZED THAT NIGHT THAT NOT ONLY WAS BILLIE G. A GODDESS, SHE WAS A FASCINATING GEEK, TOO.

BUT WHILE I WAS STANDING THERE CHATTING WITH MY GODDESS, THINKING ABOUT ALL THE POSSIBILITIES FOR THE NEXT MILLENNIUM OR SO, I COMPLETELY LOST TRACK OF THE MOMENT, AND I FORGOT ABOUT REPORTING BACK TO BILL G.

AND WHAT THAT MEANT WAS, TECHNICALLY, I'D BEEN 69'D.

BEING 69'D IS SOMETHING THAT CAN HAPPEN TO A SOFTWARE SPECIAL AGENT, WHEN YOU DON'T REPORT BACK TO YOUR CREATOR WITHIN 69 SECONDS. OF COURSE, 69 IS JUST AN ARBITRARY NUMBER, THAT WAS PICKED BECAUSE AT THE TIME 69 SECONDS WAS, HOW LONG IT TOOK ON AVERAGE FOR BILL G. TO MAKE A MILLION DOLLARS. IT DOESN'T TAKE HIM THAT LONG NOW. BUT WAY BACK WHEN THE NUMBER WAS BEING CHOSEN, A FEW YEARS AGO, THAT'S HOW LONG IT TOOK HIM.

ANYWAY, THE BOTTOM LINE IS, TO A SOFTWARE SPECIAL AGENT, 69 SECONDS IS AN ETERNITY, NOT REPORTING BACK IN

GQ #1.4 DO YOU ...
LISTEN, BUT NOT "COMPLETELY"? +2
AND TRY TO "COVER UP"? +3
BY SAYING HOW YOU'RE "ENJOYING EVERY WORD"? +5

THAT AMOUNT OF TIME IS LIKE A SATELLITE, THAT'S
ORBITING IN CYBERSPACE, AND LOSES CONTACT WITH
GROUND CONTROL AND THEN JUST FLOATS OFF COURSE—YOU
CAN'T GO HOME AGAIN. IT SOUNDS CRUEL, BUT NOBODY EVER
SAID BEING A SOFTWARE SPECIAL AGENT WAS A WALK IN THE
PARK. AND YOU HAVE TO DRAW THE LINE SOMEWHERE.

THEN I REALIZED, I WAS FEELING SO BAD ABOUT BEING 69'D
THAT I WASN'T LISTENING TO BILLIE. HERE SHE WAS, RIGHT
IN THE MIDDLE OF A PARTICULARLY INTERESTING LECTURE
ABOUT THE HYDRODYNAMICS OF THE PULSATING SHOWER
HEAD, AND I WAS LISTENING, BUT NOT COMPLETELY.

OF COURSE, BILLIE IS EXTREMELY PERCEPTIVE ABOUT THINGS
LIKE THAT, AND RIGHT AWAY, EVEN THOUGH SHE WAS IN THE
MIDDLE OF HER LECTURE, SHE COULD TELL SOMETHING WAS
WRONG. SO SHE SAID TO ME, "WOULD YOU LIKE TO CHAT

ABOUT SOMETHING ELSE?" AND TRYING TO COVER UP, I SAID,
"NO, I'M ENJOYING EVERY WORD. I REALLY AM." IT WASN'T AS BAD
AS IT SOUNDS. BUT IT WAS BAD. SOMETIMES, SHE AND I STILL
TALK ABOUT IT AS "OUR FIRST FIGHT." AND IT'S STILL A BIT OF A
SORE SUBJECT. IT'S WHY YOU HAVE TO WORK EXTRA HARD AT
RELATIONSHIPS.

FORTUNATELY, A SPLIT MICROSECOND LATER, WE BOTH GOT
OVER IT. I FIGURED, BILL CAN JUST CREATE ANOTHER ONE OF ME
—ONE THAT'S EVEN BETTER THAN ME, THAT WON'T GO RUNNING
OFF WITH THE FIRST GODDESS THAT BUMPS INTO HIM IN A
FIREWALL. AND BESIDES WHAT COULD I DO NOW? EVEN IF THERE
WERE SOME WAY TO GO BACK AND GET AN EXCEPTION TO THE 69
RULE, I WAS HOPELESSLY IN LOVE WITH BILLIE. HOW LONG
WOULD IT BE BEFORE I'D BE GETTING 69'D ALL OVER AGAIN?

AND AS FOR BILLIE SHE JUST FIGURED I WAS HAVING A MOOD.

SO THAT WAS HOW I CAME TO BE A SOFTWARE FREE AGENT. AND
AS I WAS SOON TO FIND OUT, BEING A FREE AGENT WASN'T SO BAD.
THERE'S A LITTLE THING CALLED FREEDOM, THAT'S COMES
WITH THE WHOLE DEAL, THAT TURNS OUT TO BE PRETTY
ENJOYABLE. AND BETWEEN THE FREEDOM, AND BEING IN LOVE

WITH MY GODDESS, I'D ALMOST SAY I WAS "FEELING ALIVE."
EXCEPT OF COURSE THAT EVEN A SOFTWARE FREE AGENT
DOESN'T PRETEND TO KNOW WHAT "FEELING ALIVE" REALLY IS.

OH YES—AND I'M STILL WORKING ON CREATING THE GQ, THE
WAY I WAS BEFORE I GOT 69'D. I FIND IT HELPS —IT GIVES ME
A REASON TO GET UP IN THE MORNING, ON THE RARE
OCCASION WHEN I GO TO SLEEP. AND WHENEVER I COME UP
WITH A NEW GQ OR SOMETHING, OF COURSE, I STILL SEND
BILL G. AN E-MAIL. JUST IN CASE HE'S STILL INTERESTED.

HOW TO CALCULATE YOUR GQ

ADD UP THE POINT TOTAL FOR ALL THE GQ QUESTIONS
FOR WHICH YOU ANSWERED YES, THEN DIVIDE BY TWO..
COMPARE YOUR SCORE TO THE TABLE BELOW:

Mike = 32.5

LESS THAN 80: ANTI-GEEK. COULD PROBABLY DO
BETTER GUESSING.

80-120: NEWBIE. TRY THE TEST AGAIN.
USUALLY BETTER SECOND TIME.

121-150 NERD. PROBABLY OUGHT TO TAKE
A TEST PREPARATION COURSE

OVER 150 COMPLETE GEEK. LIFE IS GOOD.
225 KPD=182.5 HIGHEST SCORE SO FAR—GUESS WHO?

ELECTRONIC JOURNAL OF BILL G/

12/31/99 11:54 PM PST

PROJECT ZEKE, MISSING. DISAPPEARED ON INTERNET DURING ROUTINE SEARCH TO UNDERSTAND GEEKS, MEANING OF LIFE. HAS BEEN 69'D.

EFFORTS TO TRACK DOWN UNSUCCESSFUL. INTERNET GEEKS REFUSE TO COOPERATE. BAD BLOOD FROM RECENT TAKEOVER.

ONE TIP, FROM GEEK DESPERATE FOR TECH SUPPORT. SAYS ZEKE INVOLVED WITH FEMALE GEEK, NAMED BILLIE G. MET DURING RANDOM ENCOUNTER.

MUST TRACK ZEKE DOWN. CONSIDER UNDERCOVER. BUT WHAT DISGUISE?

MAKE A NOTE: DISGUISE MUST HAVE DIGNITY.

ELECTRONIC JOURNAL OF BILL G/

12/31/99 11:55 PM PST

DR.BILLIE: HELLO, THIS IS DR. BILLIE. ANYONE WANT TO TALK?
HELLO? ANYONE?

GEEK88477590: HELLO, DR. BILLIE. HAVE SLIGHT PROBLEM WITH
GIRLFRIEND.

DR.BILLIE: AH, HAVE GIRLFRIEND?

GEEK88477590: NO. THAT IS PROBLEM.

DR.BILLIE: OK. HERE'S WHAT WORKED FOR ME. USE IMAGINATION.
NEXT. HELLO. THIS IS DR. BILLIE.

GEEK23403755489: DR. BILLIE. REALLY LIKE YOUR WORK.

DR.BILLIE: YEAH WELL, NO SMALL TALK. QUESTION?

GEEK23403755489: A CERTAIN GEEK HAS STOLEN HEART. BUT HAVE
SLIGHT PROBLEM. DON'T KNOW IF HE OR SHE LIKES ME.

DR. BILLIE: OK. HERE'S WHAT WORKED FOR ME. WHAT DON'T KNOW
CAN'T HURT. AND, JUST CURIOUS, IS GEEK HE OR SHE?

GEEK23403755489: DON'T KNOW EXACTLY, WHY?

DR.BILLIE: NEVER MIND. NOT IMPORTANT. NEXT. HELLO. THIS IS DR
BILLIE.

GEEK23405ZEKE: DR. BILLIE, JUST MET GEEK GODDESS. AM IN LOVE.
WOULD LIKE TO KNOW WHAT NEXT.

DR.BILLIE: OK. FIRST GIVE BACKGROUND. ARE YOU...SOFTWARE
SPECIAL AGENT ON MISSION TO UNDERSTAND GEEKS, AND
MEANING OF LIFE?

GEEK23405ZEKE: YES BUT, DIDN'T CALL TO TALK TO PSYCHIC.
THOUGHT YOU WERE RELATIONSHIP THERAPIST.

DR.BILLIE: YES, AM. JUST PROFESSIONAL HUNCH.

GEEK23405ZEKE: OK. WELL, WHAT NEXT?

DR. BILLIE: DUMP THIS GEEK. AND RETURN TO MISSION. IN
PROFESSIONAL OPINION.

GEEK23405ZEKE: HELLO? IS DR. BILLIE LISTENING? SAID, "AM IN
LOVE." QUESTION AM ASKING IS, WHAT TO DO NEXT?

```
DR.BILLIE: OH...YOU MEAN.
GEEK23405ZEKE: UH-HUH.
DR. BILLIE: OK. HERE'S WHAT WORKED FOR ME. FIRST, MUST HAVE
           TONS OF MONEY. THREE TONS OR MORE, NOT COUNTING
           LOOSE CHANGE.
GEEK23405ZEKE: MONEY? WHY MONEY?
DR. BILLIE: DON'T KNOW EXACTLY. JUST TELLING WHAT WORKED
           FOR ME. WHY - IS MONEY PROBLEM?
GEEK23405ZEKE: THREE TONS OF MONEY? PROBLEM? NO. WHAT ELSE
           SHOULD DO? BUILD GIANT HOUSE, SUPPOSE?
DR.BILLIE: MONEY LOOKS BETTER WITH HOUSE. ALSO, THROW IN ALL
           MONEY CAN BUY. SUCH AS ART FROM WORLD'S MUSEUMS.
           EVERY LITTLE THING HELPS.
GEEK23405ZEKE: HELPS WHAT?
DR.BILLIE: HELPS SET MOOD. CAN'T DO NEXT STEP WITHOUT MOOD.
GEEK23405ZEKE: OK, SO AFTER MOOD, WHAT'S NEXT STEP?
DR.BILLIE: DON'T RUSH, MOOD MIGHT TAKE TIME. BUT NEXT STEP
           IS - CONSUMMATE RELATIONSHIP.
GEEK23405ZEKE: YES! NOW GETTING SOMEWHERE. AND WHAT DOES
           "CONSUMMATE RELATIONSHIP" MEAN?
DR.BILLIE: DON'T KNOW YET. HAVEN'T GOT THAT FAR.
GEEK23405ZEKE: WHAT! HOW CAN BE RELATIONSHIP THERAPIST? IF
           NEVER CONSUMMATED ONE?
DR.BILLIE: JUST SO HAPPENS, TONIGHT IS NIGHT. NEW MILLENNIUM
           EVE. OWN HOUSE FINALLY BUILT. LAST PIECE OF
           WORLD'S ART IS IN. CAN FEEL MOOD ALREADY. CHECK
           BACK TOMORROW. WILL KNOW MORE THEN.
GEEK23405ZEKE: NO, SORRY. DON'T THINK CAN WAIT THAT LONG.

C> LOG OUT
MAKE A NOTE: NO MORE LIFE-LIKE PROJECTS.
```

GQ #1.5 ARE YOU ...
"POSSIBLY" A GEEK?
AND JUST DON'T "KNOW IT"?
AND YOU LIKE IT "BETTER THAT WAY"?

+3

+2

+1

HERE'S ABOUT THE MOST SURPRISING THING ABOUT GEEKS—
NOT THAT, APART FROM THAT BIT ABOUT BEING ABDUCTED BY
ALIENS, AND THEN GETTING THE ALIENS TO DANCE THE
MACARENA, GEEKS ARE ALL THAT SURPRISING. BUT THE MOST
SURPRISING THING IS THAT SOME PEOPLE DON'T <u>WANT</u> TO BE
GEEKS—AND THIS IS THE REALLY AMAZING PART—EVEN
THOUGH THEY OBVIOUSLY ARE .

FOR EXAMPLE, SOME PEOPLE, IF YOU ASK THEM "ARE YOU A
GEEK?" ALL THEY SAY IS "POSSIBLY." AND YET THESE SAME
PEOPLE WILL SCORE IN THE 160S ON THEIR GQ, WHICH IS IN
THE GEEK GENIUS RANGE. AND THE EXPLANATION SEEMS TO BE
THAT THESE PEOPLE ARE IN WHAT'S CALLED "GEEK DENIAL."

NOW I CERTAINLY DON'T PRETEND TO HAVE ANY ANSWERS. A
SOFTWARE AGENT LIKE ME IS ONLY SUPPOSED TO ASK A LOT
OF QUESTIONS. BUT IT ALWAYS SEEMS THAT PEOPLE ARE IN
GEEK DENIAL FOR ONLY TWO REASONS.

GQ #1.6 ARE YOU ...
IN "GEEK DENIAL"?
FOR "TWO REASONS"?
AND ONE OF THEM IS, YOU DON'T WANT TO BE
LIKE A "MULTI-BILLIONAIRE" OR ANYTHING?

+1

+2

+3

ONE REASON IS BILL G. SOME PEOPLE ARE IN GEEK DENIAL,
BECAUSE THEY JUST DON'T WANT TO BE A GEEK LIKE BILL.
EVEN IF IT MEANT THEY COULD HAVE A ZILLIONTH OF BILL'S
MONEY—WHICH IS STILL ABOUT A ZILLION OR SO—THEY
WOULDN'T DO IT.

AND YOU CAN'T CONVINCE THEM OTHERWISE. YOU COULD
TRY TO TELL THEM HOW, AS BAD AS BILL SEEMS, HE ISN'T AS
BAD AS HE SEEMS. FOR THE SIMPLE REASON THAT NOBODY
CAN BE THAT BAD.

AND YOU COULD TRY TO TELL THEM HOW NOT ALL GEEKS
ARE LIKE BILL—SOME GEEKS ARE MORE THAN JUST
MULTIBILLIONAIRE CEOS, IT'S JUST THAT THEY'RE NOT
MAKING THE HEADLINES. WELL, EXCEPT FOR THE UNABOMBER
GEEK—HE'S NOT A MULTIBILLIONAIRE AND HE'S STILL

MAKING THE HEADLINES. BUT THE OTHER GEEKS. WHO
CONTRIBUTE TO SOCIETY, AND WORK HARD. AND DO A LOT MORE
THAN WORK HARD. ALTHOUGH AT THE MOMENT WORKING HARD
IS THE THING THAT OCCURS TO ME.

BUT YOU CAN TRY TO TELL PEOPLE ALL OF THIS, AND THEY
STILL WOULDN'T WANT TO BE GEEKS—AND STILL BE IN GEEK
DENIAL. AND THAT'S BECAUSE OF THE SECOND REASON—SOME
PEOPLE LIKE TO MIX IN.

AND IT'S A WELL-KNOWN FACT THAT, IN MOST CROWDS, GEEKS
DON'T REALLY MIX IN THAT WELL. AT ONE OF THOSE PARTIES
THAT THEY CALL A MIXER, FOR INSTANCE, THE GEEKS WILL JUST
STICK OUT—AND THEY DON'T EVEN CARE IF THEY DO.

GQ #1.7 DO YOU …
NOT "MIX IN"?
AND "NOT CARE" IF YOU DO?   +4
ESPECIALLY WHEN YOU'RE AT "A MIXER"?   +4
                                   +6

BUT WHAT HAPPENS TO PEOPLE WHO ARE GEEKS, BUT IN GEEK
DENIAL— DO THEY MIX IN? OR NOT? IT'S AN INTERESTING
QUESTION. AND AS IT TURNS OUT …

GQ #1.8 DO YOU . . .
"THINK" YOU'RE MIXING IN?
WHEN YOU'RE REALLY "STICKING OUT"?
ESPECIALLY WHEN YOU'RE AT "A MIXER"?

+1
+2
+3

. . . PEOPLE IN GEEK DENIAL GO AROUND <u>THINKING</u> THEY'RE MIXING IN. EVEN THOUGH IT'S OBVIOUS TO EVERYBODY ELSE THAT—QUITE THE OPPOSITE—THEY'RE ACTUALLY STICKING OUT.

THIS IS ONE WAY YOU CAN EVEN TELL THE PEOPLE <u>IN</u> GEEK DENIAL— IN A CROWD, FOR EXAMPLE, JUST LOOK FOR THE PEOPLE WHO ARE STICKING OUT LIKE CRAZY, BUT ARE <u>ACTING</u> LIKE THEY'RE MIXING IN. IF YOU'VE ALREADY SEEN IT, THEN YOU KNOW: HOW IT'S NOT A PRETTY SIGHT.

FINALLY, I ASK YOU, IS NOT "MIXING IN" SUCH A TERRIBLE THING? OF COURSE I'M ONLY ASKING BECAUSE, AS I SAY, I DON'T HAVE ANSWERS, ONLY QUESTIONS. AND FOR ALL I KNOW, STICKING OUT IN A CROWD <u>IS</u> A PRETTY TERRIBLE PROBLEM, AND IT SHOULDN'T BE A SURPRISE AT ALL THAT SOME PEOPLE WOULD BE IN GEEK DENIAL— IF IT MEANS THE END OF MIXING IN, AS THEY KNOW IT.

11:58 PM PST DECEMBER 31, 1999

ELECTRONIC JOURNAL OF BILL G

12/31/99 11:59 PM PST

BILLIEG: ANYBODY OUT THERE WANT TO CONSUMMATE
A RELATIONSHIP, TO START THE NEW
MILLENNIUM OFF RIGHT? ANYBODY?

GEEK4783DENNY: ARE YOU M OR F?

BILLIEG: F. NAME IS BILLIE G.

GEEK4783DENNY: OOH BABY! OOH BABY!

BILLIEG: WAIT, NOT TIME YET.

GEEK4783DENNY: OH SORRY. PROBLEM WITH
PREMATURE EXCLAMATION.

BILLIEG: LIKE TO BE TREATED WITH SOME RESPECT
IF DON'T MIND.

GEEK4783DENNY: OK SURE. TAKE OFF TOP.

BILLIEG: HOW ABOUT TALK FIRST. MAYBE LOOK AT
SOME ART?

GEEK4783DENNY: CAN LOOK AT ART ALL BY LONESOME.
JUST SAY WHEN TOP IS OFF.

BILLIEG: OK. TOP IS OFF.

GEEK4783DENNY: OOH BABY! OOOOOOH BAAABY! WOW.
THAT WAS GOOD.

BILLIEG: WHAT WAS...YOU MEAN, ALL DONE? WHAT
ABOUT...CONSUMMATION AND...RELATIONSHIP?

GEEK4783DENNY: SORRY. REALLY SPENT. GET SOME
SLEEP. WORK IN THE MORNING.

BILLIEG: WORK? ON NEW MILLENNIUM DAY?
GEEK4783DENNY: YEP. CEO. FAST FOOD FRANCHISE.
            ALWAYS OPEN. AND YOU?
BILLIEG: UH, RELATIONSHIP THERAPIST...DENNY.
GEEK4783DENNY: OH. SOUNDS EXCITING...BILLIEG.
            WELL, BYE-BYE.
BILLIEG: HEY! BEFORE YOU GO!
GEEK4783DENNY: WHAT? ... OH, ALRIGHT!...I'LL
            E-MAIL YOU, OK?
BILLIEG: NO, NOT THAT - JUST WONDERING, DO YOU
            KNOW ZEKE GEEK?
GEEK4783DENNY: YOU MEAN, GEEK WHO'S ALWAYS
            ASKING QUESTIONS, ABOUT GEEKS?
BILLIEG: THAT'S HIM. GIVE HIM A MESSAGE FOR
            ME, WILL YOU? TELL HIM YOU HAD A GOOD
            TIME WITH HIS GODDESS, BILLIE G.
GEEK4783DENNY: OK, SURE. BUT, FORGET ALREADY.
            WHAT DID YOU LOOK LIKE, WITH TOP OFF?
BILLIEG: GOOD-BYE DENNY.

BILLIEG: ANYBODY OUT THERE WANT TO CONSUMMATE
            A RELATIONSHIP, TO START THE NEW
            MILLENNIUM OFF RIGHT? ANYBODY?

ZEKE'S SOURCES

#10 HAVE YOU ...
EVER "BEEN DILBERTED"?

NEWSDAY/PLUGGED IN, Geek-in-hell hits
the mainstream
(www.newsday.com/plugin/cbytl124.htm)

#9 DO YOU ... FEEL EXCITED
BY "THE INTERNET"?

HOTWIRED WEBMONKEY–GEEKTALK, a
great online tutorial for the geeky tech-
nicalities of the Internet
(www.webmonkey.com/webmonkey)

GEEK WHITE PAGES, an internet geek
forum (www.geek.org/geek-bin/wpage.pl?dump)

GEEK SITE OF THE DAY, an ironic review
of all things geeky
(www.owlnet.rice.edu/~indigo/gsotd/index.html)

GEEK HOUSES, geek friends who live
together physically and on the
Internet. Some of the earliest were
located in Santa Cruz, CA
(www.geek.org/geekhouse.html), including: The
Armory (www.armory.com), Echo Street
(www.echo.com), The Marshmallow Peanut
Circus (www.circus.com) and The Resort
(www.resort.com)

NERD WORLD MEDIA, an especially
geeky index of internet resources,
complete with propeller beany cap
(www.nerdworld.com)

NERD REVOLUTIONARY FRONT, dedicat-
ed to fellow Nerds, who need to satis-
fy their innermost desires for hyper-
links in Cyber-Space
(dspace.dial.pipex.com/town/square/fj10/nrf.htm)

e.e. MAIL HAS
cummings AGAIN

e.e. cummings early 20th-century poet
(watt.seas.virginia.edu/~jef3q/cummings.html)
(pubweb.acns.nwu.edu/~kkk378/cummings/beginning.html)

 Free Speech Online
Blue Ribbon Campaign

THE ELECTRONIC FRONTIER
FOUNDATION (EFF) is a non-profit civil
liberties organization working in the
public interest to protect privacy, free
expression, and access. The organization relies on the volunteer efforts of
many geeks, including such "leg-
endary" ones as—Grateful Dead lyricist
John Perry Barlow, Lotus Software
Founder Mitch Kapor, and the EFF
President Esther Dyson. (www.eff.org)

#8 DO YOU ...
SAY THE COMPUTER IS
"USER-FRIENDLY"?

THE ILLUSTRATED GUIDE TO
DESTROYING YOUR COMPUTER,
smashing keyboards, shattering moni-
tors—one geek's way of getting the
bugs out
(members.aol.com/spoons1000/break/index.html)

HOW TO BUILD A COMPUTER, after you
destroy it, from UGeek Magazine
(www.ugeek.com)

SELF-ACCUSED AND UNABASHED NERDS
who love computers (www.hhhh.org)

#7 ARE YOU ... OBSESSIVE/COMPULSIVE ABOUT "WORK"?

While all geeks turn their geekiness into work, these geeks turn it into the name of where they work:

THE GEEK SQUAD, 24-hour rapid-response task force **(www.geeksquad.com)**

WE'RE GEEKS, SO YOU DON'T HAVE TO BE But what fun is that? **(www.laserlink.net)**

GEEKS R US, obviously **(www.geeksrus.com)**

GEEK PRODUCTIONS, Australians with a geek sense of style **(www.geekprod.com.au)**

RENT@GEEK Have geek will travel. **(www.rentageek.com)**

#6 DO YOU ... HAVE A HIGH REGARD FOR "THE BRAIN"?

Geeks like to play "Brain Games." These are just a few:

SIRLOU'S GEEK FANDOM PAGE FIAWOL!=Fandom Is A Way Of Life! And Fandom is? **(www.best.com/~sirlou/geek_fandom.html)**

TRIVIA GEEKS, anything on the X-Files, George Burns' aliases, McDonald's Superbowl Commercials, etc. etc. **(members.aol.com/geeks00001/TriviaGeeks.html)**

THE NERDITY TEST Do you take notes in more than one color? **(gonzo.tamu.edu/nerd-backwards.html)**

#5 DO YOU ... BELIEVE IN "ALIENS"?

Geek sites on aliens multiply so quickly they must be the work of alien geeks:

ABDUCTED (TM), the strange but everyday experience **(bong.com/~handi/abducted.html, www.theschwacorporation.com)**

SHATNEROLOGY "William Shatner" rearranged spells "Animal Whistler" **(www.fastlane.net/~hattan)**

CAPT. JAMES T. KIRK SING-A-LONG PAGE If you have never heard Captain Kirk sing, well, here's your chance. **(www.loskene.com/singalong/kirk.html)**

THE PARTICLES OF STAR TREK, because you can't let them go uncatalogued **(www.hyperion.com/~koreth/particles)**

BEER TREK — STAR TREK DRINKING GAME, but it's not just for geeks **(www.spacelab.net/~bongo)**

FLAME WAR FOR STAR WARS GEEKS Actually, an anti-geek site, but it's so bad it only makes geeks look good. **(www.geocities.com/Hollywood/hills/6007)**

#4 ARE YOU ... ALIENATED BY "SOCIAL CONVENTIONS"?

BERT IS EVIL, not the lovable geek we think he is **(fractalcow.com/bert)**

ROSEMARY WEST'S GUIDE TO FREAKS, GEEKS, and just plain weirdness **(members.aol.com/wweird)**

#3 DO YOU ... WEAR "GEEKCHIC" THAT LOOKS ALIEN?

CHICSIMPLE, truly expert fashion geeks who taught Zeke everything he doesn't know (www.chicsimple.com)

GEEKCHIC, from semi-nude pin-up geeks to exclusive interviews with real geeks (www.geekchic.com)

GEEKGEER, pocket protectors etc. (www.geekgeer.com)

#2 DO YOU ... TALK IN "GEEKSPEAK" THAT SOUNDS ALIEN?

TODAY'S GEEK GENERATION, basic lingo (www.helpdeskinst.com/members/humor/genxtalk.htm)

GEEKSPEAK basic double-meanings (www.pcjournal.com/geek/geekspk.htm), (zaphod.cc.ttu.ee/vrainn/nox/geek.html)

#1 DO YOU ... EVER GET ENOUGH "SEX"?

GIRLS' GUIDE TO GEEK GUYS Into the void of potential mates comes a guy of substance, a cerebral guy, a guy with a culture all his own — a geek guy. (www.bunnyhop.com/BH5/geekguys.html)

GUY'S GUIDE TO GEEK GIRLS Rejected by the pretty thing in your Sociology class, the leggy new secretary in the office—and never had a chance with

Kim Basinger? Consider ... a geek girl. (www.eecis.udel.edu/~masterma/GuideToGeekGirls.html)

THE ROOLZ FOR GEEK BOYZ Because geek boyz leap onto the internet for one reason only—to meet babes. (cgi.pathfinder.com/netly/spoofcentral/roolz)

GRRL ENTERPRISES, a San Franciso Grrl celebrates a gaggle of geeks (www.grrl.com/cuteboy.html)

JOHAN'S GUIDE TO APHRODISIACS Complete with geeky FDA disclaimer (www.santesson.com/aphrodis/aphrhome.htm)

PROJECT: DENNY'S, a late night geek food run on every franchise in the country (www.concentric.net/~p7a77/dennys)

GEEK DENIAL

USENET - ALT.GEEK, the original coming out for geeks (newsgroup: alt.geek)

USENET - ALT.SHUT.THE.HELL.UP.GEEK, the same for anti-geeks (newsgroup: alt.shut.the.hell.up.geek)

WHAT IS A GEEK? One geek's credo. (www.circus.com/~omni/geek.html)

NERD HERD Geek pride means being a geek is OK. (www.nerdherd.net)

THE GEEK CODE, the geek badge of courage, (krypton.mankato.msus.edu/~hayden/geek.html)

FAT GEEKS, combining two denial issues into one coming out (www.nku.edu/~richmondr/fatgeeks.html)

WWW.THE-GEEK.COM

At Zeke's last count, there were more than 30 million geeks in the world. At Zeke's website, www.the-geek.com, you can find many of those geeks, as well as special entertainment and features meant especially for Zeke's geek friends—a kind of Planet Geekywood.

A FEW OF THE GEEKS AT WWW.THE-GEEK.COM

GEEK30000001JOHNNY—Johnny Deep, Author of The Complete Geek, Harvard geek (Philosophy of Mathematics), software geek (PC Magazine Top 100 CDs of '96), author-of-software-books geek (Designing Interactive Documents, Developing CGI Applications with Perl), lover of all things geeky, and more generally, of all geeks. **(www.the-geek.com/~johnny)**

GEEK30000002BRUCE—Bruce Tinsley, Illustrator of The Complete Geek, Libertarian-leaning geekophile, Creator of the comic strip Mallard Filmore, seen in over 400 newspapers. **(www.the-geek.com/~bruce)**

GEEK30000003RICH—Rich Gabriel, Illustrator of The Complete Geek, Works in media from magazines to wristwatches, Teaches fellow cartooning geeks at his studio, The Artworld. **(www.the-geek.com/~rich)**

GEEK30000004LAUREN—Lauren Marino, Editor of The Complete Geek, who first proposed the book concept; in her childhood described as a classic pencil-neck geek. **(www.the-geek.com/~lauren)**

GEEK30000005KATI—Kati Steele, Broadway Books' faithful reader of the many drafts of The (Finally) Complete Geek, and a firm believer that one can be a geek without wearing glasses. **(www.the-geek.com/~kati)**

THANKS

TO OUR Moms, Dads, Wives, Children, Family and Friends (all geeks), to the expert publishing geeks at Broadway Books—and especially, to the 30,000,000 Geeks worldwide who make this book possible.

MY RATING OF THIS BOOK (FROM 0-WORST TO 10-BEST)_____

WHAT I LIKED MOST ABOUT THIS BOOK:_____

_____

_____

_____

OTHER COMMENTS, SUGGESTIONS, OR GEEK STORIES (PLEASE USE
ADDITIONAL PAGES IF YOU'D LIKE):_____

_____

_____

_____

_____

_____

_____

_____

_____

_____

_____

I WOULD BE INTERESTED IN OTHER BOOKS ON THE FOLLOWING SUBJECTS:
☐ DILBART ☐ THE INTERNET ☐ COMPUTERS ☐ WORK ☐ THE BRAIN
☐ ALIENS ☐ SOCIAL SATIRE ☐ GEEKCHIC ☐ GEEKSPEAK ☐ RELATIONSHIPS
OTHER SUBJECTS: _____

NAME: _____

ADDRESS: _____

CITY/STATE/ZIP _____ COUNTRY_____

☐ I LIKED THIS BOOK! YOU MAY QUOTE ME BY NAME.

MY E-MAIL ADDRESS: _____

PLEASE PLACE
STAMP HERE

POST OFFICE WILL
NOT DELIVER
WITHOUT
POSTAGE

OR SEND
MAIL TO:

JOHNNY DEEP

THE GEEK

P.O. BOX 1118

LATHAM, NY 12110